STEPS ALONG THE WAY

Steps
Along the Way

LUIS PALAU

KINGSWAY PUBLICATIONS
EASTBOURNE

ISBN 0 86065 332 3

Unless otherwise indicated, biblical quotations are from
the New International Version, © New York International
Bible Society 1978.

RSV = Revised Standard Version
copyrighted 1946, 1952, © 1971, 1973 by the
Division of Christian Education of the National
Council of the Churches of Christ in the USA

First published as a series in
Christian Herald, the family weekly, 1983

Cover photo: The J. Allan Cash Photolibrary

Printed in Great Britain for
KINGSWAY PUBLICATIONS LTD
Lottbridge Drove, Eastbourne, E. Sussex BN23 6NT by
Richard Clay (The Chaucer Press) Ltd, Bungay, Suffolk.
Typeset by Nuprint Services Ltd, Harpenden, Herts.

Contents

Introduction

Dear Christian friend,

Welcome to the family of God! Your decision to commit your life to Jesus Christ is the most important decision you will ever make.

The moment you made that decision, you became a new creation in Christ (2 Corinthians 5:17). You received new life in him (1 John 5:12).

Now it's time to start growing. We all start out as spiritual babies, but we shouldn't stay that way! Like any child, we need four elements to grow—food, love, rest and exercise.

1. Spiritual food

If we are to become mature in Christ, we need to feed on God's word and pray. The Bible is God's instruction book for living. Prayer is our chance to talk with the Lord of the universe.

Discover how Bible reading and prayer can revolutionize your daily life. I recommend that you immediately start reading in the Gospel of Luke in the New Testament. Read just one chapter a day at first and talk to God about what you learn.

2. Love

Every child needs love as he grows. Spiritually, we need to remember and rejoice that God loves us (John 3:16; Romans 5:8). Nothing can separate us from his love (Romans 8:37–39).

In addition, God gives us Christian love through fellowship in a good local church. Regularly attend a good Bible teaching church where you find an atmosphere of love and acceptance.

3. Rest

As Christians, we also need to rest by turning our problems, anxieties and fears over to Christ (Matthew 11:28–30; 1 Peter 5:7). When you rest in Christ, you will still be tempted (just as I am), but you can overcome temptation by the power of Christ who lives in you (1 Corinthians 10:13; Galatians 2:20). The most important lesson you can learn in the next few months is to rest in the living Christ!

4. Exercise

Finally, in order to grow to maturity, every child needs exercise. Spiritual exercise involves telling your relatives, friends and acquaintances about your new life in Christ, and taking an active part in the ministry of your local church (Romans 12:1–8; Ephesians 4:11–16).

Again, let me welcome you to the family of God. As a fellow brother in Christ, I rejoice with you! I pray that this book will encourage you and help you to grow in your walk with Jesus Christ.

As the father of four growing boys, I know that babies aren't babies forever. They start crawling, then taking a few wobbly steps, and eventually walking and growing up. A similar maturing process should slowly be taking place in our lives spiritually with every step we take. In the pages that follow, let's consider some of these 'steps along the way' to Christian maturity.

Your brother in Christ,

Luis Palau

P.S. May I ask you to do a special favour for me? Write and tell me how you came to know Christ. (I have included my own testimony at the end of this book, incidentally.) Writing your own story is good practice and will make it easier to tell others about your new life in Christ. Receiving your testimony will be a special encouragement to everyone associated with our team as we hear how God is changing lives in Britain today!

Luis Palau Evangelistic Team Europe
175 Tower Bridge Road
London SE1 2AS

STEP 1

Taking Time to Pray

What is the greatest sin in Britain? Is it adultery? Greed? Vice? Murder? Alcohol abuse?

May I suggest *prayerlessness*?

How often, and with what regularity, do you receive answers to prayer? Many Christians have no idea what it is like to talk to God with a real need and then receive a specific, valid and recognizable answer to their prayer.

I could tell you Bible promises on prayer, plus some of my own experiences, and those of my friends, but I can't do your praying for you. You can read all of the books on prayer, and listen to others pray, but until you begin to pray yourself you will never understand prayer. It's just like riding a bicycle or swimming. You learn by doing.

Martin Luther said,

> Just as the business of the tailor is to make clothing, and that of the shoemaker to mend shoes, so the business of the Christian is to pray.

The secret of Luther's revolutionary life was his commitment to spend time alone with God every day.

'Consider the lives of the most outstanding and shining servants of God,' J. C. Ryle challenges us, 'whether they be in the Bible or out of the Bible. In all of them you will find that they were men of prayer. Depend on prayer; prayer is powerful!'

I encourage you to take time every day to talk with

God. Don't just give him thirty seconds while you're rushing around in the morning—'Oh Lord, bless this day, especially since it is Monday...' What kind of prayer is that?

It is essential to set aside a specific time each day for personal prayer. Strive for order and faithfulness, but avoid legalism. On certain occasions you may need to select a different time during the day to pray. Nothing is wrong with that. But aim for consistency.

I have found that the early hours of the day are the best to pray. So have such men of God as Martin Luther, John Wesley, Robert Murray M'Cheyne, George Müller, Hudson Taylor and Andrew Murray. D. L. Moody echoed their sentiments when he said:

> We ought to see the face of God every morning before we see the face of man. If you have so much business to attend to that you have no time to pray, depend upon it that you have more business on hand than God ever intended.

Make room in your schedule to begin each day alone with God in prayer.

On the other hand, prayer is something that should take place during the entire day. The Bible says, 'Pray continually' (1 Thessalonians 5:17). At any moment, whatever the occasion, we are free to speak with our Father. Al Wollen has said that every Christian can enjoy 'constant, conscious communion with God'. We enjoy this communion with the living God who lives within us through prayer.

'If Jesus prayed, what about you? What about you?' asks the hymn writer. It's always surprising to see how much time Jesus dedicated to prayer. He never considered himself too busy to pray. As the obligations increased and as he faced big decisions, he went away alone to pray.

What about you?

STEP 2

Praying in God's Will

What is your favourite Bible promise? Is it a promise for strength? Courage? Security?

Let me share one of my favourite Scripture promises with you.

> This is the assurance we have in approaching God: that if we ask anything according to his will, he hears us. And if we know that he hears us—whatever we ask—we know that we have what we asked of him (1 John 5:14–15).

Look at that! God has gone on record as saying that whatever we ask for according to his will, he will give to us.

'There's only one problem, Luis,' you say. 'I don't know God's will. What good is this promise if I can only guess at his will?'

Fortunately, God has revealed much of his will to us in the Bible.

By becoming better acquainted with God's word you will learn many things about his will for your life. His will is not hidden; it is revealed and written! Instead of speculating about God's sovereign will for tomorrow, we should focus on obeying his revealed will today. 1 John 5:14–15 promises that God will give us whatever we ask so that we may do his will. This includes a measure of God's wisdom (James 1:5) and strength (Isaiah 40:29–31).

If you are not sure a prayer request is according to

God's will, ask him about it. He can tell you! Don't worry about making mistakes when you pray. Do you think the sovereignty of God will be shattered just because you make a mistake in praying? Isn't it a bigger mistake not to pray at all?

If the answer to your request is 'No', the Lord will soon communicate the answer by the internal witness of the Holy Spirit. If you walk with God and have a consistent prayer life, then a sensitivity develops between you and your heavenly Father.

If God gently says 'No' to a request you make, then he has something even better in store for you. Jesus says, 'If you, then, though you are evil, know how to give good gifts to your children, how much more will your Father in heaven give good gifts to those who ask him!' (Matthew 7:11). If we ask for a worthless stone, he says 'No' and gives us nourishing bread instead. God always gives us what is good. Isn't that a promise worth claiming?

We only begin to experience the enthusiasm, joy and excitement of the Christian life as we claim God's promises through prayer.

STEP 3

Prayer God Answers

D. L. Moody, the great nineteenth-century evangelist, visited the British Isles frequently during his many years of ministry. God used Moody to help bring two continents to repentance. It is estimated that he travelled over one million miles and preached the Gospel of Jesus Christ to over 100 million people.

What characteristics made Moody stand out as God's man to reach the masses in North America and Europe? He was a man of *faith*. He was a man of *purity*. And he was a man of *prayer*. Moody asked God to move the mountains of unbelief in the souls of men—and God answered!

Moody had this to say about prayer: 'Some men's prayers need to be cut short at both ends and set on fire in the middle.' Are your prayers on fire? Are they prayers that reach the ear of God? Are they prayers that move the hearts of men?

Let me briefly describe the kind of prayer God delights to answer. If you take these principles to heart, watch for God to anoint your prayers with fire.

First, we must *believe*. Do you believe God is able and willing to answer your prayers? 'I'm sure he is able,' you say, 'but I'm not so sure he is willing.' Hebrews 11:6 says,

> Without faith it is impossible to please God, because anyone who comes to him must believe that he exists and that he rewards those who earnestly seek him.

Prayerlessness is a problem, but as much a problem is disbelief, which includes Christians who don't believe God will answer their prayers. No wonder their prayers lack any fire! The Bible clearly teaches that God answers prayer offered in faith.

Second, we must ask. 'You do not have, because you do not ask God' (James 4:2). Do you remember the story of the blind man in Mark 10? He was extremely excited about meeting Jesus. When they met, Jesus asked him, 'What do you want me to do for you?' Jesus wanted to be asked! God wants to pour out his blessings—if we will only ask. The blind man came right to the point. 'Lord, I want to see.' He didn't beat around the bush as we often do. We try to twist God's arm with our long detailed petitions and explanations. What we need to do is cut off the flowery words and get to the point. That sets our prayers aflame.

Third, we must *confess* sin. The psalmist wrote, 'If I had cherished sin in my heart, the Lord would not have listened' (Psalm 66:18). Sin douses the flames of prayer. Unconfessed sin extinguishes more prayers than we could imagine.

King Saul was anguished when he realized at the end of his life that God wasn't answering his prayers (1 Samuel 28:6). He let unconfessed sin build a wall between himself and God. Is anything standing between you and God? If so, confess your sins and experience the renewal of God at work in your life again.

Moody preceded each of his evangelistic campaigns by urging God's people to pray. The fires of revival that swept the British Isles were not lit by Moody alone. They were ignited by the prayers of 'ordinary' Christians who believed God, confessed their sins, and then offered prayers God delighted to answer.

STEP 4

Praying with Expectancy and Thankfulness

You may have started to wonder if I will talk about anything else besides prayer. I will! But I feel an urgency to impress you as my brothers and sisters in Christ with the importance and joy of practising consistent, daily prayer.

Someone once remarked: 'If I wished to humble anyone, I should question him about his prayers. I know nothing to compare with this topic for its sorrowful self-confessions.'

The last thing I want to do is make someone simply feel guilty about not praying. Guilt is Satan's bitter substitute for action in the Christian life. Instead, God wants you to experience joy in your daily Christian walk. That is why Scripture encourages us to pray.

The Bible says, 'Devote yourselves to prayer, being watchful and thankful' (Colossians 4:2). We should offer our requests with expectancy and thankfulness. We miss the joy of seeing prayer answered if we do not consciously watch for signs of God's intervention.

I encourage you to start a prayer notebook as a means of watching for God's answers to your prayers. Keeping a prayer notebook always motivates me to pray more frequently and specifically, and it helps me to sense the reality of my personal relationship with God.

First I write my request down in a notebook along with the date I start making the request. If there is a deadline for a particular answer I record that as well. Then in the other column I write down when the Lord answers my prayers, and what his answers are. It is exciting to see how God works!

My prayer notebook is a monument of the constant faithfulness of my heavenly Father. When I encounter difficult circumstances, I can reflect on God's faithfulness by reviewing how God has worked in my life in the past. Without a notebook, I would soon forget many of God's marvellous answers to my prayers.

To start your own notebook, complete the exercise in prayer outlined below. Then rejoice as you experience God's personal dealings in your life!

Exercise in Prayer

1. Think of one area in your life where you really need an answer to prayer.
2. Write it down and date it. Develop a prayer notebook.
3. Study the following passages in your Bible on prayer: Matthew 7:7–11; 18:19–20; Mark 10:46–52; John 16:24; Romans 8:26–27; Ephesians 6:10–20; James 5:13–18.
4. Simply and specifically tell the Lord what your request is.
5. Picture the answer in your mind.
6. Thank the Lord that he is going to answer (Philippians 4:6).
7. Each time the answer to prayer comes to mind, thank the Lord for his answer.
8. Record the answer when it comes and praise God (Colossians 4:2).

How is your prayer life? You don't need to give a sorrowful confession. Instead, offer your requests with expectancy and thankfulness. Use a prayer notebook to help you. Then share your blessings with others. Be a living testimony that God still answers prayer!

STEP 5

Talking with God

'Prayer is friendship with God,' according to James M. Houston. I think he has made an important observation. Prayer is simply two friends talking together.

Prayer is a conversation between God and ourselves. It isn't a one-sided, one-track monologue of petitions, but a well-rounded dialogue. God speaks to us through his word and the inner witness of the Holy Spirit. We respond to God with *adoration, confession, petition, intercession* and *thanksgiving*. Without these five elements our prayers become lopsided, disproportional, askew. Let's consider these five aspects of prayer together briefly.

The first element of true prayer is *adoration*. As we enter God's presence in prayer, we begin by expressing our worship and reverence for him. The Talmud gives this dictum: 'Man should always first utter praises, and then pray.' We find the praises of our Lord from past generations recorded throughout the pages of Scripture.

Confession follows our praise. When Isaiah saw the Lord in his glory he cried: 'Woe to me! I am ruined! For I am a man of unclean lips' (Isaiah 6:5). We cannot praise the God of holiness without developing a deep sense of our own uncleanness. The Bible also teaches us that God graciously forgives us when we confess our sins (1 John 1:9).

Only after adoration and confession do we offer our *petitions* to the Father. True prayer consists of the petitions of one who acknowledges his utter need, and the provisions of one who demonstrates his utter goodness. Jesus gives us this promise:

> Until now you have not asked for anything in my name. Ask and you will receive, and your joy will be complete (John 16:24).

He encourages us to ask the Father for what we need.

As we pray we should also include *intercession* for others. What a ministry we can have at the throne of grace on behalf of others! The prophet Samuel told the people of Israel, 'Far be it from me that I should sin against the Lord by failing to pray for you' (1 Samuel 12:23). Intercession for others is an important spiritual responsibility we must not neglect as Christians.

Thanksgiving should naturally fill the remainder of our conversation with God. Listen to these exhortations from the apostle Paul:

> Be joyful always; pray continually; give thanks in all circumstances, for this is God's will for you in Christ Jesus (1 Thessalonians 5:16–18).

We experience God's joy when we talk with him in prayer and thank him for his answers. The great evangelist Charles Finney noted, 'when God wants to bless his people, he first moves them to pray.' He moves them to converse back and forth in a well-rounded dialogue. Has God moved you to pray? Let's stop and talk with him right now.

STEP 6

Communion with God

Some years ago a doctor asked an elderly Christian woman in England, 'If I asked God for five pounds, would I get it?' The old lady answered with a question. 'If you were introduced to the Prince of Wales, would you ask him for money at once?'

'No, not until I knew him better,' replied the doctor.

'Well,' remarked the old lady, 'you will need to know God a great deal better before you can expect him to answer your prayer.' Someone commented on this incident, 'Many people presume to ask God for things upon mere acquaintance with him.' Isn't that often the case?

Prayer, as we said before, is simply two friends talking together. The Bible is God's side of the conversation. When I read the Scriptures, I soon find myself whispering a petition. When I pray, God's word comes to mind. When I listen to his word, my soul bows in adoration.

The great Bible expositor W. Graham Scroggie wrote: 'In the Bible God speaks to us; and in prayer we speak to God.' They are intertwined strands forming the intimate cord of communion between God and ourselves.

Read the great prayers of Moses, Nehemiah, Ezra and Daniel. In their petitions they spoke God's words back to him. This is the prayer language God delights to answer. As you pray, let him bring Scriptures to mind. Pray them back to God as they apply to you.

Before you spend time reading and studying the Bible each day, pray that God will make your heart sensitive to his word. Martin Luther said, 'Having prayed well, is having studied well.' We cannot have one without the other.

George Müller communed with God as few men in history have ever done. Through him, God cared for thousands of British orphans. Despite his tremendous financial responsibilities, Müller never spoke to others about his needs. Extreme financial situations only motivated him to spend more time in intimate conversation with God. Listen to what Müller said about his times alone with God: 'I begin to meditate on the New Testament early in the mornings.... Invariably, I have found that...after so many minutes of meditation, my soul is guided to confession, or to give thanks, or to intercede, or to make a request. So, even when you couldn't say that I had given myself to prayer, but rather to meditation, nevertheless, it turned out that almost immediately the meditation turned into prayer.'

As God's word spoke to Müller's heart, he naturally responded back to God in prayer. He enjoyed intimate conversations with his Lord.

Communication is the key to any relationship. Our relationship with God can only grow as we communicate our adoration, confession, petition, intercession and thanksgiving to him through prayer, and as we listen to his voice through the daily study of his word.

How well do you know God? How intimate is your relationship with him? Müller could come to God as a close friend, ask him for five pounds, and know God would somehow supply his need. Could you ask God for that, or are you only an acquaintance still?

STEP 7

How Authoritative is the Bible?

Biblical authority is one of the oldest and most discussed questions among men. It is also one of the most important for us to consider today. Men often prove their spiritual condition by their attitude toward the Bible.

Several years ago I had the opportunity to meet about a dozen ministers near a city where I was involved in a crusade. To say I was shocked by our discussion may be a bit strong; however, I was quite surprised by the serious differences of opinion we had on some basic questions. At least half of these ministers did not accept the Bible as the authoritative word of God! Several commented that they believed there were passages in Scripture that were erroneous. Even more astonishing was their admission that when they are uncomfortable with portions of the Bible they rationalize away such portions because they are 'unscientific'.

Is it any wonder that in certain parts of the world the Christian church staggers? Who wants to listen to ministers who don't believe the Bible as the word of God? Where is their authority? Where do you draw the line between which passages of the Bible are inspired by God and which are not?

When I hear people who profess to be Christians questioning whether the Bible is God's word, I can't help but wonder if Christians today worship too small a God. After all, if God is God, then couldn't he write a book that was without error? Of course he could, and he did! Paul could confidently tell Timothy:

But as for you, continue in what you have learned and have become convinced of, because you know those from whom you learned it, and how from infancy you have known the holy Scriptures, which are able to make you wise for salvation through faith in Christ Jesus (2 Timothy 3:14–15).

Why could Paul say that? Because all Scripture is inspired by God; it is authoritative because it is *God's* word, not man's. Peter could write:

We did not follow cleverly invented stories when we told you about the power and coming of our Lord Jesus Christ, but we were eye-witnesses of his majesty (2 Peter 1:16).

The Bible rings with authenticity. No other book has this divine stamp of approval.

Arthur T. Pierson, a noted Bible expositor explained the Bible's uniqueness this way:

From all human oracles, however self-confident, we turn at last to the inspired Word where, instead of ambiguous and untrustworthy utterances, we find teachings distinct and definite, authoritative and infallible.

We can trust God's word!

If God can't write a book that is perfect, then why should you or I trust such a God with our salvation? I do not want to suggest that belief in inspiration is necessary for salvation. But for us to experience authority and power and communion with God in our Christian walk, we must accept the Bible as God's word. Belief in the full authority of Scripture is vital to our understanding of the authentic and victorious Christian life. It is only through such faith that we can begin to conform to the image of Christ.

STEP 8

Reaffirming the Bible's Authority

Many people today attack the authority of God's word. They throw out certain passages and question many others. How should we respond to such attacks?

The great preacher Charles Spurgeon responded this way: 'Defend the Word of God? Might as well defend a lion.' It doesn't need any defence. We can confidently follow the footsteps of godly men throughout the ages in acknowledging the Bible's authority.

Christ himself recognized the Scripture as God's word. He made a point of quoting supposedly controversial or 'hard-to-believe' passages in the Old Testament just to attest their historical accuracy. Jesus referred to the creation story (Matthew 19:4–6; Mark 10:2–9; 13:19), Noah and the flood (Matthew 24:36–39; Luke 17:26–27), and Lot and the cities of Sodom and Gomorrah (Matthew 10:15; Luke 10:12; 17:28–30). Jesus even referred to the Old Testament account of Jonah (Matthew 12:40–41; 16:4). Many people today laugh at the story of Jonah and shrug it off as a fairy tale or bedtime story for little children. Why? Because according to what knowledge they have of science, it is impossible, they reason, for a whale to swallow a man and then vomit him alive out of his belly after three days.

First of all, the Bible doesn't say Jonah was swallowed by a whale, but rather a great fish (Jonah 1:17). More importantly, the historical account is recorded in the Bible, and Jesus said it happened. If Jesus believed it, why shouldn't we believe it too? I like the comment Dr Billy Graham once made when someone used the Jonah story to 'prove' the Bible was fictitious. Dr Graham said that if God was God, then not only could the fish have swallowed Jonah, but if God wanted, Jonah could have swallowed the fish!

The Bible clearly states, 'All Scripture is God-breathed' (2 Timothy 3:16). John R. W. Stott explains the importance of this declaration for us:

> The meaning then is not that God breathed into the writers, nor that he somehow breathed into the writings to give them their special character, but that what was written by men was breathed by God. He spoke through them. They were his spokesmen.

The very words of Scripture are inspired by God. Someone has wisely observed, 'You can as easily have music without notes, or mathematics without figures, as thoughts without words.' Inspiration applies to every part of the Bible and to the Bible as a whole—not just to the 'thoughts' it conveys to a reader.

Jesus said,

> I tell you the truth, until heaven and earth disappear, not the smallest letter, not the least stroke of a pen, will by any means disappear from the Law until everything is accomplished (Matthew 5:18).

He guarantees even the most minute parts of it!

The early church fathers also asserted the authority of the Bible. Augustine declared,

> Let us therefore yield ourselves and bow to the authority of the Holy Scriptures, which can neither err nor deceive.

Why should we cower before the attacks of certain critics of the Bible? As believers we need only submit to God and his authoritative word. Scripture is the standard by which we should measure everything else.

STEP 9

The Word of Life

Why was the Bible written? To explain the complexities of human government? To criticize certain theories of economics? To teach us the wonders of astronomy?

My friend, the purpose of the Bible is not to tell us how the heavens go, but how to go to heaven. The Bible's great message is that God desires to transform radically the lives of men and women through his word, preparing them for eternity with him in glory.

God's word has power to transform individuals from condemned sinners to redeemed believers. I know. A British gentleman, Frank Chandler, brought me to saving faith in Jesus Christ by reading Romans 10:9–10 to me. I was only 12 years old when I sincerely committed my life to Christ through prayer, but from that moment on I knew I was a child of God. I knew I was going to heaven when I died. Christ had paid for my sins by his death on the cross.

Conversion—the transformation of an individual from a sinner to a child of God—is impossible apart from God's word. British missionaries brought God's saving word to Argentina where I grew up. My father is in heaven because of their work. My grandmother is in heaven because of their work. Millions of people around the world—including myself—thank God for the British missionaries who brought them God's word.

The Bible has power to transform anyone anywhere—the high or low, the rich or poor, the educated or illiterate. I have even had the privilege of seeing the President of a certain country in South America come to know Christ personally. He told me, 'Palau, I'm a military man. I have done things I could never tell you about. If you knew what I was really like, you would never say God loves me.'

I replied, 'I don't want you to tell me what you've done. Jesus Christ came to save and transform men and women just like you.' Even though he was a gentleman of high position and military rank, he bowed his head and opened his heart to the Lord Jesus Christ there in his presidential office. Even when this President lost his office two years later during a revolution, he continued to go on for the Lord. He recently said, 'My life has been changed since the day when I gave my life to Christ.'

I have seen the word of God transform the lives of many, many people: the secretary of a national communist party, an illiterate janitor, a minister, a businessman, a divorced woman. The Bible is the saving word of life for people of every type—including people just like you and me.

STEP 10

The Cleansing Word

A high government official travelled to Great Britain during the late nineteenth century and was presented to Her Majesty Queen Victoria. This official asked a very significant question while visiting the Queen: 'What is the secret of England's greatness?'

The Queen sent for a beautifully bound book and presented it to the official with this statement: 'This is the secret of England's greatness.' She gave him a Bible.

Can you imagine that? Think of the startled look of the official, but the Queen was right. Britain was called 'Great' because of the tremendous influence of the Bible on her people.

We cannot reflect long on Britain's Christian heritage before we recognize that her heroes of the faith—William Tyndale, William Carey, John Knox, John Wesley, Hudson Taylor, George Müller, Robert Murray M'Cheyne and many others—were convinced of the cleansing power of God's word.

The Bible has the power to transform a new or weak Christian into a triumphant maturing man or woman of God. That work is known as sanctification. The Bible frees us from sin, cleanses us and makes us holy in our walk before God.

The Lord Jesus prayed to his Father in the garden of Gethsemane: 'Sanctify them by the truth; your word is truth' (John 17:17). His word cleanses us (John 15:3). It isn't enough to know that the Scriptures 'are able to make you wise for salvation through faith in Christ Jesus' (2 Timothy 3:15). Paul goes on to say in verse 16: 'All Scripture is God-breathed *and is useful for teaching, rebuking, correcting and training in righteousness.'*

I find that the word immediately points out the little sin spots on the altar of my soul. Dusty Bibles lead to dirty lives.

Why do some countries actively strive to keep the Bible out of the hands of their people? An embassy official in Czechoslovakia made this statement:

> Drugs are just an ordinary crime. Bibles, however, are political. Drugs affect the body, but Bibles affect and influence the mind. To the Communist officials, that is very serious.

In Britain, in contrast, 600,000 Bibles are freely purchased each year for private use and as gifts. It is estimated that 84% of the householders in Britain own a Bible, and 71% of adult individuals have their own personal copy. We enjoy free access to many versions of the Bible in our own language today.

William Tyndale lived in a day when no one had an English Bible. It was forbidden in Britain. Tyndale dreamed of seeing his country transformed and cleansed by the word of God. He dedicated his life to translating the Scriptures into English. Before the age of 45 he was burned at the stake for attempting to make his dream come true.

The English Bibles you and I have the privilege and freedom of reading today were baptized in the blood of translators who knew the power of God's cleansing word. Dare we neglect that cleansing word today?

STEP 11

Daily Bread

Great Britain has produced some of history's most influential evangelical leaders, holy men and women 'filled with God's Spirit', who were mightily used to extend God's kingdom. Robert Murray M'Cheyne was such a leader.

Born in 1813 in Edinburgh, M'Cheyne died at the young age of 29. Yet in his short lifetime, because of his holiness, humility, sensitivity to God, unfaltering devotional life, compassion, simple preaching and love for the Bible, he made a lasting impression on society. He faithfully pursued the Lord's work.

To me, the most outstanding characteristics about M'Cheyne were his holiness, humility and anxious efforts to save souls. The need for personal holiness before God so impressed him that he once wrote in a letter:

> According to your holiness, so shall be your success.... A holy man is an awesome weapon in the hand of God.

Many factors bring revival to a nation or a community but holiness among the people of God—particularly among the leadership—is fundamental. Sin, a lack of holiness, grieves the Holy Spirit and hinders his work. Scripture warns, 'Do not grieve the Holy Spirit' (Ephesians 4:30) and 'Do not put out the Spirit's fire' (1 Thessalonians 5:19).

On the other hand, Scripture exhorts us, 'Be filled with

the Spirit' (Ephesians 5:18). To be filled with the Spirit is a command, a duty and a privilege for the Christian. To be filled with the Spirit means to be walking in the Light and controlled by the indwelling Lord. To do this you must spend time every day reading and studying in the Bible, filling your mind and your heart with the life-changing inspired word of God (Colossians 3:16).

In 1843, just weeks before he died, M'Cheyne published a Bible reading plan, 'Daily Bread', to help his congregation get to know the Bible 'in all its breadth'.

Today, Scripture Union publishes helpful devotional guides by that same name.* They give a Bible reading for every day and cover most of the New Testament and the major passages of the Old Testament in four years. Short comments show how God's word relates to the problems of today. I highly recommend that you use such a guide as a systematic plan for your daily Bible reading.

One of my earliest memories is of sneaking out of bed early in the mornings to watch my father go into his small office. There he knelt alone to read the Bible and pray before going to work. That made a deep impression on me as a child.

One day my dad told me that he read a chapter from Proverbs every day, since it has 31 chapters and there are 31 days in most months. I still try to practise that suggestion even now. In spite of all the other Bible studying and reading I do, I try to start the day with my chapter from Proverbs. And I have learned to do it on my knees.

What about you, my friend? Have you disciplined yourself to read from the Bible each day? If not, start today! Begin in the book of Proverbs and then find a Bible reading programme you can follow to read the whole Bible through. Don't let 24 hours go by without partaking of your daily bread.

* *For more information write to: Scripture Union, 130 City Road, London EC1V 2NJ.*

STEP 12

Studying the Bible for Yourself

Do you enjoy studying the Bible on your own? Are you
satisfied with your ability to apply biblical truths to daily
living?

Christians sometimes neglect to study their Bible
because they lack a simple, practical method that makes
Bible study come alive for them. But we cannot grow and
mature spiritually unless we eat regularly from the Bread
of Life. One Christian leader stated:

> I cannot too greatly emphasise the importance and value of
> Bible study... in these days of uncertainties, when men and
> women are apt to decide questions from the standpoint of
> expediency rather than on the eternal principles laid down by
> God himself.

Bible study starts with *observation*. Our observations of
any object—including the Bible—are directed by the
nature of the object to be studied. We observe stars by
looking at them through a telescope night after night. We
observe animals' behaviour by watching them over a long
period of time in their natural habitat. We observe the
Bible as we would any book—by carefully reading it
frequently.

The noted Bible teacher Dr James M. Gray declared:

> There is only one law of Bible study, and that is to read the
> Book, and when you have read it, to read it again, and then sit
> down and read it once more, and by and by you will come to
> *know* the Book.

Read the book of the Bible you are studying at one sitting. Philippians or James are good books to study at first. Get a clear impression of the book as a whole. Disregard chapter and verse divisions. Read it again and again, occasionally using various translations to get a better grasp of its message. Ask probing questions: Who? What? When? Where? Why? How?

After observing the text, *interpretation* follows. We must guard against allowing our presuppositions to bias our interpretation. Pray for the Spirit's enlightening; apart from his illumination, proper understanding is elusive (1 John 2:20, 27).

Examine the context of the passage you are interpreting. Also compare the passage with parallel accounts and cross references. Charles Spurgeon remarked:

> Nowadays we hear men tear a simple sentence of Scripture from its connection, and cry, 'Eureka! Eureka!' as if they had found a new truth; and yet they have not found a truth diamond, but a piece of broken glass.

The best Bible commentary is the Bible itself. But Bible handbooks, dictionaries and a good atlas help us understand better the biblical lands, customs and history. Consult them when needed, being careful not to spend a great deal of time reading about the Bible without ever turning to God's word for yourself.

Finally, seek to *apply* God's word to your life. You haven't done this unless it changes your behaviour. Relate the Bible to all areas of your life—your strengths and weaknesses, attitudes and actions. What does it say to you as a son or daughter, parent or child, employee or employer? James tells us:

> Do not merely listen to the word, and so deceive yourselves. Do what it says (James 1:22).

Obey the word by prayerfully meditating on it with a view to better understanding and application.

Observation. Interpretation. Application. These three simple steps are your key to open the door for exciting Bible study!

STEP 13

Memorizing God's Word

Warning:

> *Authorities have determined that Scripture memorization may be hazardous to your spiritual health.*

Dawson Trotman, founder of the Navigators, once asked a young man how much Scripture he knew. He said he had memorized 1,500 verses.

'You mean you could quote 1,500 verses to me right now?' Trotman asked incredulously.

'That's right,' the young man said with obvious pride.

Trotman replied, 'I wish you could only quote five verses—*but lived them!*' This young man only had head knowledge of Scripture, not heart application.

Many years ago, the village priest in Kalonovaka, Russia, took a special liking to a pug-nosed lad who recited his Scriptures with proper piety. By offering various inducements, the priest managed to teach the boy the four Gospels, which he recited nonstop in church one day. Sixty years later, he still liked to recite scriptures, but in a context that would have horrified the old priest. The prize pupil who memorized so much of the Bible was Nikita Krushchev, the former Communist tyrant.

John W. Alexander, president of Inter-Varsity Christian Fellowship, gives us this warning:

> There is little merit inherent in the mere process of memorizing Scripture. One could memorize voluminous portions and be an atheist. Satan memorized enough to use it to tempt Jesus.

Alexander goes on to add, however,

> Memorizing *is* helpful when we yearn for Scripture to energize our whole lives.

Warning:

> *Authorities have also determined that Scripture memorization can greatly enhance your spiritual vitality.*

What makes the difference, my friend, between superficial and beneficial Scripture memorization? I believe it's prayerful meditation. Memorization in itself may sharpen our intellectual capacities, but that's about all. Memorization with a view to meditation helps us think straight in a crooked world. The Bible says,

> Whatever is true, whatever is noble, whatever is right, whatever is pure, whatever is lovely, whatever is admirable—if anything is excellent or praiseworthy—think about such things (Philippians 4:8).

How can we think on what is pure when we are confronted daily with impurity? By purposefully meditating on God's word. We can't read the Bible all day, but we can always meditate on passages of Scripture—if we have memorized them. After 24 hours, research shows, we accurately remember five per cent of what we hear, 15 per cent of what we read, 35 per cent of what we study, but 100 per cent of what we memorize.

Let me suggest five tips for memorizing Scripture that I think you will find helpful.

1. Read the verse at least ten times.
2. Write it 20 to 30 times slowly as you think about each word.
3. Practise quoting it; it should be easy by now.
4. Meditate on it throughout the day and review it on subsequent days.

5. Share the verse with others as you converse together.

My friend, I strongly encourage you to start memorizing Scripture passages—and meditating on them. But let me warn you: it may change your life!

Scripture passages that have changed my life

If you don't already have an established Scripture memorization plan, start with the verses I have listed below. I have memorized and meditated on all of these passages, and they have made a big difference in my life. I know they will in yours as well!

New Birth
- [ ] 1. Salvation (John 3:16)
- [ ] 2. New Life (2 Corinthians 5:17)
- [ ] 3. Identity as God's children (1 John 3:1–2)
- [ ] 4. God lives in you (1 Corinthians 6:19–20)
- [ ] 5. Baptized into one Body (1 Corinthians 12:13)

God
- [ ] 6. Christ as the Word (John 1:1)
- [ ] 7. The Spirit of God (John 15:26)
- [ ] 8. Counsellor (John 14:16–17)
- [ ] 9. God's strength (Ephesians 6:10–11)

Family
- [ ] 10. Wives (Ephesians 5:22)
- [ ] 11. Husbands (Ephesians 5:25)
- [ ] 12. Children (Ephesians 6:1–3)
- [ ] 13. Parents (Ephesians 6:4)

Growth
- [ ] 14. Temptation (1 Corinthians 10:13)
- [ ] 15. Confession and forgiveness (1 John 1:9)
- [ ] 16. Prayer (John 14:13–14)

☐ 17. Meeting together (Hebrews 10:24–25)
☐ 18. Loving one another (John 13:34–35)
☐ 19. Freedom from Legalism (Colossians 2:20–22)

God's Word

☐ 20. Authority (2 Peter 1:20–21)
☐ 21. Purpose (2 Timothy 3:16–17)
☐ 22. For our purity (Psalm 119:9, 11)

Victory

☐ 23. Walk in the Spirit (Galatians 5:16–17)
☐ 24. Dedication and transformation (Romans 12:1–2)
☐ 25. Victory through the Cross (Galatians 2:20)
☐ 26. The Fruit of the Spirit (Galatians 5:22–23)
☐ 27. The Great Commission (Matthew 28:18–20)
☐ 28. Death and resurrection in Christ (Romans 6:3–4)

The Future

☐ 29. Eternal condemnation (Revelation 21:8)
☐ 30. Heaven (John 14:1–3)

Discipline yourself to learn one verse or short passage every week (memorize faster if you wish). Mark off each verse as you learn it.

But don't stop there! Meditate on them. Say them over in your mind occasionally throughout the day. Keep asking: *So what? What difference should this make in my life?*

Pray that you will not only be able to hide each verse in your head, but also in your heart so that God can use it to change your life (Psalm 119:11). Ask God to help you hear what he is trying to say to you through his word.

STEP 14

Claiming God's Promises for Yourself

As you have read and studied, memorized and meditated on various passages in the Bible, what sections have seemed the most difficult to believe? Prophecy? Narrative portions? Doctrinal passages? Or God's promises?

I have a hunch many Christians have the most problem believing the promises of God. Oh, they sound nice. Sometimes they even cheer us up. But we wonder, 'Do they really work?' Unconsciously, at least, we question whether God keeps his promises or not.

D. L. Moody confidently stated, 'God never made a promise that was too good to be true.' Think about that!

In the Old Testament we read, 'Not one of all the Lord's good promises to the house of Israel failed; every one was fulfilled' (Joshua 21:45; compare 23:14–15). Solomon later declared, 'Praise be to the Lord who has given rest to his people Israel just as he promised. Not one word has failed of all the good promises he gave through his servant Moses' (1 Kings 8:56). None of God's promises have ever failed! The only absolutes we can set forth are those found in God's word. The Bible testifies of things beyond that which man knows or can learn apart from God's revelation.

God has gone on record numerous times throughout his authoritative word and given his people 'very great and precious promises' (2 Peter 1:4).

Some of his promises were made specifically to an individual (Joshua 14:9) or a group (Deuteronomy 15:18) or even a nation (Haggai 1:13). We must be careful not to haphazardly claim promises intended for someone else!

Many Old Testament promises, thankfully, are repeated in the New Testament and are ours to claim today. God promised to Joshua, 'I will never leave you or forsake you' (Joshua 1:5). In Hebrews 13:5 God transfers that promise to us as Christians. Charles Spurgeon stated:

> O man, I beseech you, do not treat God's promises as if they were curiosities for a museum; but believe them and use them.

We appropriate God's promises by learning them (through study and memorization), by seeing our need for them and by giving God time to appropriate them into our daily experience. Dr J. I. Packer said,

> God teaches the believer to value his promised gifts by making him wait for them, and compelling him to pray persistently for them, before he bestows them.

God has promised to meet our every need. But we must ask for his provision. Christ says, 'Ask, and it will be given to you; seek and you will find; knock and the door will be opened to you' (Matthew 7:7). Any of God's promises that we can claim in Jesus' name are guaranteed and will be performed for us by God for his glory (John 14:13–14; 2 Corinthians 1:20).

What is the need of your heart today, my friend? The Lord has promised to meet that need! Take him at his word. God has something special in store for you!

STEP 15

God's Promises When We Hurt

Several years ago a submarine sank, with all its crew, off the Atlantic coast of North America. The vessel was eventually located and frogmen went down to assess the damage and the possibility of salvaging the wreck. As the divers neared the hull of the vessel they were surprised to hear the pounding of a message in Morse code. It was evident that someone was actually still alive in the submarine. The message was a frantic question beat against the walls of the aquatic tomb: 'Is there hope? Is there hope?'

You and I ponder that same question when a particular problem or tragedy strikes us. Who, after all, is totally free from the crushing pain of losing a loved one, or the frustration of unemployment, or the anguish of a fragmented home, or any of a hundred other problems? We feel trapped and submerged by the weight of our circumstances and wonder, 'Is there hope? Is there really any hope of overcoming this problem?'

We often remember Romans 8:28 in such times—'And we know that in all things God works for the good of those who love him, who have been called according to his purpose.' Vance Havner commented, 'Paul did not say, "We understand how all things work together for good," he said, "We know that they do".' That promise is a solid anchor when the storms of life beat heavily against us.

The apostle Paul had claimed that very promise many times before he ever penned his famous letter to the

Romans. He knew what it was to suffer hardship, persecution, indifference, betrayal, loneliness, ill health, stonings, beatings, shipwreck, nakedness, destitution, sleeplessness, immense pressure. What kept Paul from going under? I believe it was his utter confidence in the God who promises to sustain us no matter what. At the end of his life he could say, 'I know whom I have believed, and am convinced that he is able to guard what I have entrusted to him for that day' (2 Timothy 1:12). What had Paul entrusted to God? His very life.

In the Old Testament we read, 'Thou dost keep him in perfect peace, whose mind is stayed on thee, because he trusts in thee' (Isaiah 26:3 RSV). That promise applies to us even today, as the New Testament repeatedly reveals.

Are you facing a difficult problem today, my friend? Commit yourself anew to the Lord. Then take the words of Philippians 4:6–7 to heart: 'Do not be anxious about anything, but in everything, by prayer and petition, with thanksgiving, present your requests to God. And the peace of God, which transcends all understanding, will guard your hearts and your minds in Christ Jesus.' When the storms of life seem overwhelming, God wants us to experience his perfect peace.

O Father, we praise you that you understand our every sorrow and tear. We acknowledge our insufficiency to handle life's problems in our own strength. May your grace abound to meet our deepest needs. Sustain us as we wait upon you. Fill our hearts with your peace that passes all understanding. Thank you for your rich provision for us this day. Amen.

STEP 16

Why Does God Allow Suffering?

A philosopher from Paris once commented: 'God is dead. Marx is dead. And I don't feel so good myself.' His attitude illustrates the pessimism rampant in our culture today.

If there really is a God, people wonder, *why has he allowed so much suffering in the world?* Many Christians honestly struggle with that same question. Only by turning to the Bible can we begin to understand the problem of suffering.

Basically, there are four types of suffering. The first type is that which comes as the result of natural disasters, such as an earthquake or a large storm. The suffering that results from these disasters happens to the righteous and unrighteous (Matthew 5:45).

A second type of suffering can be called man's inhumanity to man. War would be classified under this type of suffering. Because of man's greed and pride, he tries to hurt his fellow man (James 4:1–2).

A third type of suffering is best seen in the life of Job in the Old Testament; it came as a result of Satan's attack on him. After receiving permission from God, Satan moved in and caused incredible suffering to Job and his family.

?
WHY

A fourth type of suffering is that which comes as a result of our own erroneous actions. For example, if I walk off the roof of an office and fall to the ground, breaking my leg, I am suffering because I broke God's law of gravity. Individuals also suffer when they break God's moral laws.

Much suffering can be traced to the evil choices men make. Some—not all—suffering is allowed by God as a punishment for sin. Often God simply forces men to live with the consequences of their actions (Galatians 6:7–8).

Whenever men break God's laws, others are bound to suffer as well. I refer you to the story of Achan in Joshua 7. When he coveted some of the spoil from the battle of Jericho, his sin cost the lives of 36 men in the battle against Ai. It is inevitable that others will suffer in the wake of an individual's disobedience.

How we respond to suffering—whether we brought it on ourselves or not—is either going to make or break us as Christians.

Circumstances often do more to reveal our character than to shape it. But by properly responding to trials we can develop patience and a proven character (Romans 5:3–4).

Problems, stress, calamity or the death of a loved one often cause us to search ourselves for any sin in our lives (see 1 Kings 17:18). Pain plants the flag of truth in a heavy heart. But we must be cautious not to let Satan overwhelm us with excessive and false guilt or grief (2 Corinthians 2:7). Job's wife told him to curse God and die. He refused to give up and remained faithful to God. Notice in the end God gave him all that he had before and more (Job 42:10–17).

Instead of looking at our circumstances, we need to keep our eyes on Jesus Christ who is the source of life. He will bring us through whatever situation we face and as a result we will be stronger Christians, better able to serve him because of our trials.

In a day of pessimism and suffering we can say with the psalmist, 'The Lord is with me; I will not be afraid. What can man do to me?' (Psalm 118:6). The Lord himself—as the great Sufferer—is our comfort and hope in troubled times.

STEP 17

Maintaining a Proper Perspective

Did you know that there is enough moisture in a single cup of tea to blanket your entire neighbourhood with fog 15 metres thick? It's amazing how such a small amount of water—spread out so thinly—can hinder our vision almost completely. We tend to get upset when fog hinders our travel but we forget the sun is still shining overhead, burning it away. Why do we get upset? Because we fail to maintain a proper perspective.

The great statesman William Wilberforce once commented,

> The objects of the present life fill the human eye with a false magnification because of their immediacy.

Problems and concerns often act like fog to obscure our present situation. They keep us from seeing things in perspective.

Psychologists tell us that 45 per cent of what we worry about is past, and 45 per cent is future. (Thirty per cent concerns our health alone.) Only one in every ten things we worry about will ever come to pass—and we usually cannot do anything about it anyway.

No wonder Jesus Christ tells us, 'Do not worry about tomorrow, for tomorrow will worry about itself' (Matthew 6:34). The Bible also says, 'Do not be anxious about anything' (Philippians 4:6). We worry whenever we fail to maintain a true perspective of our circumstances.

Sometimes we treat problems and trials as if we were on a television quiz show. We rush around thinking we have to solve everything in 30 seconds. When we can't, we panic.

We try every option we can think of to overcome our problems and difficulties. When none of them work, we reluctantly turn to God as a 'last resort'. But there are no emergencies in heaven. God is aware of our problems (Exodus 3:7; 1 Peter 5:7). He did not create us to be self-sufficient to meet these needs. He created us to depend on him.

A. W. Tozer wrote,

> The man who comes to a right belief about God is relieved of ten thousand temporal problems, for he sees at once that these have to do with matters which at the most cannot concern him for very long.

Do you face a difficult situation, my friend? Has your way been covered by a heavy fog? God has not allowed this situation to come into your life to discourage or defeat you. Every trial you and I face is an opportunity for God to demonstrate who he is to us—*a loving and faithful heavenly Father*.

King Hezekiah saw God demonstrate his care for him in a dramatic way. Meditate on Isaiah 37 and record the steps King Hezekiah took when faced with a serious problem. Then compare your list with mine below.

1. Hezekiah acknowledged he had a problem (37:1).
2. He sought to know what God's word said about his problem (37:2–7).
3. He didn't allow anything to distort his perspective (37:8–13).
4. He prayed to God: first worshipping him, then presenting his request, and finally asking that God would be glorified (37:14–20).

Use these same steps when you face a difficulty or trial. Remember that it is in those hard places where we get to know him better.

STEP 18

Facing Death

One of the most difficult trials each of us will face is the death of a loved one. It is hard to keep things in perspective when death strikes so close to home, isn't it?

Modern man strives frantically to prolong life and secretly attempts to overcome its power. Scientists and doctors continue to develop extraordinary measures to keep the sick and dying alive just a little longer through drugs, transplants and machines.

But death continues harvesting its fruit without prejudice towards age, race, social level or education. Death continues to be cynical, cruel and real. No one escapes its cold fingers. Our appointment is sure. Neither money, fame nor intelligence exempts us from death; everyone succumbs.

How should we respond as believers when a dearly loved Christian relative or friend eventually dies?

Shortly before my father died he suddenly sat up in bed and sang a chorus about heaven. Then he fell back on his pillow and said, 'I'm going to be with Jesus, which is far better.'

My father had committed his life to Christ nine years earlier and was confident that he would spend eternity with the Lord. He was 36 years old when he went to glory; I was only 10 at the time. He died just hours before I returned home from a term at boarding school. I had no way of knowing what had happened as I stepped off the train that day and ran home. But as I neared my house I could hear weeping. My relatives tried to intercept me as I ran through the gate and up to the house; I brushed past them and was in the door before my mother even knew I was back. Tears filled my eyes when I saw my father's expired body lying in front of me.

I felt completely devastated by my father's death. My world seemed shattered and confusing. I was angry at everything and everybody. *It isn't fair,* I thought. *Why couldn't my dad die in old age like other dads?*

A British missionary delivered the message before my father's burial the next morning. It was only then that I felt complete assurance that my father was in heaven.

Oh, I still missed my dad terribly. I still felt the pangs of grief. But I rested in the hope that I would see him again one day.

Grief is a normal part of facing the death of a loved one. We do grieve at the death of other believers, but not as those who have no hope (1 Thessalonians 4:13).

Jesus gives us these words of comfort:

> Do not let your hearts be troubled. Trust in God; trust also in me. In my Father's house are many rooms; if it were not so, I would have told you. I am going there to prepare a place for you. And if I go and prepare a place for you, I will come back and take you to be with me that you also may be where I am. (John 14:1–3).

This is our blessed hope as believers!

Yes, the grieving process is absolutely normal for our emotional and physical well-being. But as Christians we do not have to be swallowed up in that grief or allow anger or bitterness to take root in our hearts. We can face it with hope, realizing it is not the end. Death is merely earth's door to heaven.

STEP 19

Beyond Death's Door

Death haunts man. Poets, philosophers and other writers throughout the ages have sought to explain, understand and cope with death.

Ernest Hemingway lived obsessed with the idea of death. His father, an intellectual, had killed himself when Hemingway was only a child. As a result, Hemingway wanted to demonstrate to all humanity that he feared neither life nor death. Ironically, when he was 61 years old, he committed suicide in a moment of rage and human weakness.

The Bible recognizes the inevitability of physical death. In Hebrews 9:27 we read, 'Man is destined to die.' In a sense, everyone is terminally ill. Unless Christ returns in our lifetime, we will all die.

Longfellow succinctly observed, 'The young may die, and the old must.' Physical death is the most stubborn and persistent enemy of humanity. But it is not the most dangerous foe.

The Bible distinguishes between physical death (which everyone eventually faces) and spiritual death (which everyone initially experiences). Death basically means separation from something or someone. It implies loneliness. Man begins life separated from God and spiritually dead because of his sin.

Sartre, the famous French existential philosopher, accurately observed, 'Man is alone.' Apart from a personal relationship with and commitment to God, man is spiritually dead and very alone.

The Bible also mentions eternal death or 'the second death' (Revelation 29:14). This is eternal, irreversible separation from God. Anyone who refuses to commit his life to Jesus Christ during his lifetime here on earth will experience this eternal death.

Physical death clearly is *not* the end of man's existence. The question is where you and I will spend eternity—in heaven or hell. There is no other option. The reality of death and hell should motivate us as Christians to share the gospel of Jesus Christ with the unconverted. Approximately 150,000 people die every day around the world. Most pass into a Christless eternity. History frequently records their agonizing last words when they realize that by rejecting Christ they are left without hope.

Voltaire, the noted French infidel, once stated: 'In twenty years, Christianity will be no more. My single hand shall destroy the edifice it took twelve apostles to rear.' Yet when he faced death he cried, 'I am abandoned by God and man!' Voltaire's doctor expressed astonishment at the emotional torment his patient experienced before passing into eternity. In contrast, the great evangelist John Wesley declared on his deathbed, 'The best of all is, God is with me.' He died satisfied and content to be in the presence of his Lord.

Death need not haunt us as Christians. If we have committed our lives to Jesus Christ, we have a glorious future awaiting us beyond death's door.

STEP 20

Reason for Living

More than 11,000 people tried to commit suicide during the past 24 hours. According to a report from the United Nations, 1,000 of these people succeeded in taking their lives. And a high percentage of these suicides were among young people.

Several years ago a high school friend of one of my sons put a gun to his head and shot himself. He was 16, the son of a wealthy and notable doctor. He had not been exhibiting any unusual outward signs of stress. But one day he came home from school and began calling some of his classmates to tell them he was going to kill himself.

'The guys didn't believe him,' my son told me. 'They thought he was joking.' An hour later this young man proved they were wrong. Why? Partially because his friends failed to respond properly when he called them. They apparently believed several myths about suicide.

One popular myth about suicide is that if someone talks about killing himself, he really won't do it. The fact is they *do* talk about it, usually with up to ten other people, before attempting to take their life.

Sometimes people simply write a note and then kill themselves. But most people talk about it first. They may have specific plans about killing themselves, but they want to be rescued instead. Perhaps that is why most suicide attempts, though serious, are not successful. People just want to know someone cares about them. Suicide is their immature way to get that attention.

Another myth about suicide is that if you mention the word 'suicide' to someone you notice is emotionally distraught or unstable, you will put the thought in his mind. That is false.

Suicides are increasing at alarming rates among all classes and types of people. A recent study on suicide revealed this surprising fact: psychiatrists have the highest suicide rate of any professional group!

Many people readily turn to Christians when they are contemplating suicide. If a friend or acquaintance causes you to think he or she may be suicidal, take the time to meet him as soon as possible.

Don't be fooled by the myths about suicide. Maybe your friend has never even thought about suicide. But don't be afraid to ask about it.

If your friend says he is thinking about killing himself, take him seriously and act quickly to get him to someone who can help him. Don't let him out of your sight, especially if he has a specific plan for killing himself (method, place, time). Suicide is not a joking matter.

Why do people attempt suicide? There are many reasons: seeking to get attention, desire to join a dead relative, anger that is internalized, loss of meaning in life, poor health, loneliness.

Make it a priority to reach out and help others in your circle of friends and acquaintances *before* the trials and difficulties of life overwhelm them. We all need a strong, supportive group of friends.

Jesus Christ came that we all might have life to the full (John 10:10). Let's tell those who are perhaps quietly but seriously searching for meaning and purpose about him—our reason for living! Let's show those who struggle with alienation and loneliness that someone really cares.

STEP 21

The Elijah Syndrome

A 55-year-old woman threw herself from her 14th floor apartment to the ground below. Minutes before jumping to her death, she saw a workman washing the windows of a nearby building. She greeted him and smiled, and he smiled and said hello to her. When he turned his back, she jumped. On a very neat and orderly desk, she had left this note: 'I can't endure one more day of this loneliness. My phone never rings! I never get letters! I don't have any friends!'

Another woman who lived just across the hall told reporters: 'I wish I had known she felt so lonely. I'm lonesome myself.'

You and I are surrounded by lonely people.

Who experiences loneliness and despair? The person living anonymously in a crowded city certainly. But also the foreigner. The rich and miserly. The divorcee and single parent. The young person. The businessman. The unemployed. No one is immune from loneliness.

Even godly men and women sometimes experience loneliness. Elijah stands out in the Old Testament as God's most dramatic, forceful prophet. He stopped the rain, challenged a king face to face, produced fire from heaven, ordered hundreds of false prophets executed and accurately predicted the day a three and one half year drought would end. Yet in the New Testament we read, 'Elijah was a man just like us' (James 5:17). Thus, he also experienced times of loneliness and despair.

By taking four wrong steps Elijah found himself under a tree in complete discouragement (1 Kings 18:46—19:4). *First*, he exhausted himself physically. *Second*, he became upset emotionally. *Third*, he failed to turn to God spiritually. *Fourth*, he isolated himself socially.

In the end he collapsed under the tree in a desert place and cried: 'I've had enough, Lord! Take my life. I just feel like dying.'

Have you ever felt completely discouraged—without anyone near to encourage you? Have you ever experienced the Elijah syndrome? Notice how God met each of Elijah's needs in his time of crisis. Physically, God gave him nourishment and sleep. Emotionally, God made his presence known to Elijah and encouraged him. Spiritually, God exhorted Elijah to once again follow him. Socially, God told Elijah about a large number of godly men and women with whom he could fellowship and receive further encouragement.

God wants to meet your particular needs as well. You cannot live the victorious Christian life alone and on your own. It's impossible. We only experience victory by the power of the indwelling Christ (Galatians 2:20). His presence and power are particularly evident when two or three gather together (Matthew 18:20).

Use your loneliness or discouragement as a motivation to commit yourself anew to the Lord. Don't sit under the tree of despair any longer. The last thing Christ told us was that he would always be with us (Matthew 28:20). He wants to be our best friend. You never have to feel alone again.

Join in also with God's people (Hebrews 10:25) and stop trying to face the daily battles of life by yourself. Pray together with others about mutual needs and concerns. Experience God at work in the Body of Christ. Victory in the Christian life is always a team effort.

STEP 22

The Sexual Counter-revolution

'My husband is overseas,' a woman told me. 'He has been gone now for nine months and will be gone for seven more. I'm very lonely and I desire affection and love. I am a Christian, but I realize that I am very weak. How can I overcome sexual temptation?'

How would you counsel this woman?

There are no easy answers. The desire for love and affection reaches deep into the soul. Loneliness also touches the human heart deeply. No one experiences it as acutely, perhaps, as someone who is separated from a spouse because of military service, work, divorce, disability or death. Sexual desires only seem to increase when one's spouse is gone for some length of time.

The Bible speaks very clearly concerning sex outside marriage. But sometimes our sexual desires feel at odds with those scriptures. The recent 'sexual revolution' boldly proclaimed that the biblical imperatives concerning sex only within marriage were outdated and invalid today. Proponents of the sexual revolution said that if you were lonely and desired affection, you had a *right* to have those needs met through an illicit affair. Trying to rationalize their feelings, people thought perhaps it was all right to commit immorality in certain circumstances. Trial marriage, group sex, spouse swapping and other sexual 'experiments' became increasingly popular.

But some proponents now regret their efforts to promote the sexual revolution. One of them, George

Leonard, recently admitted, 'What I have learned is that there are no games without rules.' People can try to break God's moral laws, but they will always have to pay the consequences. Leonard cites a *Cosmopolitan* survey in which 106,000 women confirmed that a revolution in sexual attitudes and behaviour had taken place on both sides of the Atlantic. But how did the women feel about the revolution? Most were disappointed, even disillusioned, with 'the emotional fruit the sex revolution has borne.' The survey report openly suggested 'there might be a sexual counter-revolution under way.'

The Bible clearly warns us not to be deceived for God will not be mocked.

> A man reaps what he sows. The one who sows to please his sinful nature, from that nature will reap destruction (Galatians 6:7–8).

The destructive harvest of our society's sexual promiscuity—herpes and other venereal diseases, emotional scars, desertion and spiritual shipwreck—has been a high price to pay for the momentary pleasures of sowing to the flesh.

Scripture tells us to resist the satanic sexual revolution by committing yourself to God (James 4:7). Confess your sins and draw near to him. Persevere under temptation by remembering that God always provides a way of escape (1 Corinthians 10:13).

Whether you are single or married, divorced or widowed, God understands your particular temptations and needs. Trust him to supply 'all your needs according to his glorious riches in Christ Jesus' (Philippians 4:19). No matter what everyone else may be doing, take God's eternal word to heart. Start your own sexual counter-revolution today.

STEP 23

Learning about Love, Marriage and Sex

I was only 12, but I felt like a man. School was finished for the summer and I was helping with the family business. The work was a refreshing break from my recently completed exams.

This particular day I was helping deliver a load of cement bags. The driver, a 20-year-old labourer, seemed friendly and boosted my ego as we worked together.

'Luis,' he said as we pulled over to the side of the road, 'since you are becoming a young man now and you have no father, you need someone to talk to you about the facts of life.'

My heart began to pound. I was excited to think that I might get some straight answers from someone who really knew the score. But instead of telling me anything, the truck driver simply opened a magazine and turned the pages while I stared at the pictures of naked men and women in unbelief. I was shocked and disgusted.

Later, I could not push the images from my mind. I felt sinful, degraded, horrible, guilty. Impure thoughts invaded my mind. I had been curious before, but had always resisted the temptation to look at such magazines. Now one was thrown at me unexpectedly and I was repulsed.

It wasn't until I was 23 that a man talked to me plainly from the Bible about sex. I was amazed by how much the Bible actually says about sex.

I think it's a crime that as Christians we leave sex education to other people and institutions which usually teach only about the physical aspects of reproduction and anatomy. We need to understand and teach what God says about the total spectrum of love, marriage and sex.

1. The Bible teaches that God created sex.
God made Adam and Eve as perfect, sexual beings (Genesis 2:18–25). Not until after the Fall did Satan tempt men to misuse and abuse the gift.

Often adults communicate to their children by their stubborn silence that sex is somehow evil. That's false! Sex, in my opinion, is one of the most beautiful gifts God has given humanity.

2. The Bible shows that God created sex for pleasure as well as for reproduction.
God's word exalts the joys of marital love. See the Song of Solomon, for example. Scripture likewise speaks of children as a special blessing from the Lord (Psalm 127:3).

3. The Bible presents sex as wholesome and right only within marriage.
Hebrews 13:4 says,

> Marriage should be honoured by all, and the marriage bed kept pure, for God will judge the adulterer and all the sexually immoral.

According to a recent survey by National Opinion Polls, by the age of 21 only six per cent of young people in Britain are still waiting for God's ideal—sex only in marriage. God's beautiful gift has been made trivial, distorted and cheap in so many cases.

How were your own views of love, marriage and sex formed? Are they consistent with what the Bible teaches? In an age of confused immorality, we need to personally study and understand what God says about wholesome sexuality.

STEP 24

Avoiding a Mid-life Crisis

Scripture always strikes me as true to life. It never glosses over unpleasant facts. The Bible helps each of us understand and deal with our problems because it discusses frankly the problems of those who have gone on before us.

King David, for example, started out well for the Lord. He zealously served God as a young man. Even when he had to run month after month for his life, he remained true to God's commandments. But as David reached middle age, he encountered three perils which caught him off guard (2 Samuel 11). Each of us will also face these same perils at some point in our life. If we fail to respond properly to these perils, we will experience what psychologists call a 'mid-life crisis'.

What are these perils? The first is *the peril of growing weary*. David experienced this weariness after years of fighting against the enemies of Israel. Instead of attacking the Ammonites with his army as he should have, David decided to stay home one spring and relax in Jerusalem (2 Samuel 11:1).

Weariness hits when you've been out in the working world some fifteen to twenty years. You've been married, maybe, for just as long. And life becomes very routine. Weariness easily convinces us at this point to take it easy for a change.

Second, with weariness comes *the peril of carelessness*. No one wakes up on a Monday morning and says, 'Hey, I think I'll wreck my marriage today.' But how often we hear of Christian couples who separate after twenty years of marriage. Why? Because they were careless.

58

Carelessness starts in your thought life. You drift into the ways of the world in the literature you read, the films you see. Then you get careless spiritually. Perhaps you abandon your morning Bible reading and prayer time. 'Ah, I've been getting too legalistic in my devotions,' you say. Your sensitivity level drops and Satan moves in.

David became careless when he relaxed in Jerusalem. Late one afternoon while walking upon the roof of his house David happened to see a woman bathing (2 Samuel 11:2). He allowed his eyes to gaze upon Bathsheba and dwell upon her beauty. The man after God's own heart became dangerously careless.

Third, with carelessness comes *the peril of confusion*. David failed to follow the spiritual compass of God's word and the Holy Spirit. He inquired about the woman and before the night was over committed adultery (2 Samuel 11:3–4).

When you are young you know just where you want to be when you reach 40. Then you get there and feel trapped by your responsibilities, your job, your marriage. What do you do when Satan offers you a tantalizing 'change of pace'? How should you respond to the perils of middle age?

Take a few moments and read 2 Timothy. It's a very short letter. In this epistle the apostle Paul explains how to avoid a mid-life crisis. 'Timothy,' Paul says, 'don't give up. Persist. Shun youthful lusts. Be steady. Continue in the things you have learned. Fulfil your ministry.'

As you read 2 Timothy, write down all the ways Paul mentions to resist Satan's temptations to relax and become careless spiritually. Also observe the images Paul uses to describe this steadfastness—a single-minded soldier, a disciplined athlete, a hard-working farmer, a faithful workman, a persistent fighter, a never-say-quit runner.

When you face the perils of weariness, carelessness and confusion—whether you are middle-aged or not—don't pray for an easier life. Pray to be a stronger man or woman of God.

STEP 25

Wrestling with Unemployment

Who do you know that is out of work? Someone in your family? A friend? Perhaps you have even wrestled with unemployment recently.

I wrestled with unemployment while supporting my widowed mother and five younger sisters in Argentina. In those days there were massive strikes in my home country. I was without work, without relief, without anything!

Wherever unemployment strikes, it creates unique marital, financial and even medical problems. It also prematurely exposes someone to the perils usually associated with middle age: weariness, carelessness and confusion. These very terms describe many of the unemployed in Britain today.

First, accept your unemployment—even though it may be difficult—and trust God to work it for good. The Bible tells us that

> in all things God works for the good of those who love him, who have been called according to his purpose' (Romans 8:28).

Second, carefully plan how to use your extra time in the best way possible. In Ephesians 5:15–16 we read,

> Be very careful, then, how you live—not as unwise but as wise, making the most of every opportunity.

What should a committed Christian do if he finds himself out of work? I believe the Bible gives us several specific principles that relate to the issue of unemployment.

If you are an unemployed Christian, then I suggest you should spend the first two hours of every day in Bible study and prayer. Spend the next three or four hours seriously looking for a job.

Third, minister to others during your spare time. Organize a Bible study with others who are unemployed and pray together. Spend time making disciples of new believers.

As an individual or a group, volunteer your afternoons to work for your church, help those in need, visit the elderly or actively evangelize in your community.

God's word says,

> Let us not become weary in doing good, for at the proper time we will reap a harvest if we do not give up (Galatians 6:9).

I believe God will compensate those who volunteer to help others if they do it for his glory.

Fourth, be a good steward of your time, energy and possessions. Work together as a family to see how you can creatively use what you already have to meet some of your needs, and even help others. Perhaps you have some land. Plant a garden! Perhaps you have certain talents which could be used to earn some money. Use them!

In Matthew 6:33 we read,

> But seek first his kingdom and his righteousness, and all these things will be given to you as well.

As we honour God in every part of our life we can be sure he will supply everything we need.

If unemployment strikes your home, I challenge you to seek God's kingdom and righteousness. Act on the principles outlined above and trust God to provide your every need.

STEP 26

Whatever Happened to Sin?

Billy Staton slipped a tape recorder in his shirt before going to pick up his daughter for a picnic, planning to tape his ex-wife's hostility about his visitation rights.

Instead, Staton recorded his own death in what one prosecutor called 'twenty-three minutes of murder'. Paul Wolf, 21, was charged with Staton's murder. The tape conclusively revealed that Wolf committed the murder. But he pleaded *innocent* to the slaying.

Wolf's lawyer, explained to the jurors that his client was innocent due to diminished responsibility. He said Wolf had a difficult childhood with a mentally ill mother and a hard-driving father, then faced an on-going series of custody problems after his marriage to Staton's ex-wife. The attorney explained that Wolf did not plan the killing, but was *forced* to slay Staton 'at the last minute after the steady, lengthy, continual build-up of the pressure'.

Such lawyers fill our court records day after day with excuses for their clients' actions. But no matter what the courts decide, such men and women must live with their heavy burden of guilt.

In our society, some lawyers and psychologists have tried to replace personal responsibility for sin with scientific sounding explanations for wrong-doing. Whatever happened to sin?

O. Herbert Mowrer, a noted psychologist, has stated:

For several decades we psychologists looked upon the whole matter of sin and moral accountability as a great incubus, and acclaimed our liberation from it as epoch making. But at length we have discovered that to be 'free' in this sense, that is to have the excuse of being 'sick' rather than sinful, is to court the danger of also being lost.

Another noted psychologist, Rex Julian Beaber, said this in a recent article:

> The force of evil has disappeared from nature; sinfulness is no longer man's fate. The new 'sciences' of sociology, psychology and psychiatry have cast aside such concepts as will, will power, badness and laziness and replaced them with political and psychological repression, poor conditioning, diseased family interaction and bad genes. One by one, human failings have been redesignated as diseases.

Beaber counters this modern trend by stating, 'Ultimately, we *must* assume responsibility for our actions.' Sin must be rediscovered once more in our generation.

If you scratch under the surface, most people carry burdens of guilt that nobody else knows about. We secretly hide this guilt as a skeleton in the closet of our soul. On the advice of our psychiatrist, we deny its existence. We explain it away. We repress it. We do anything but admit our failure. Ironically, until we make such an admission our closet full of guilt will continue to haunt us.

Rudyard Kipling said it well, 'Nothing is ever settled until it is settled right.' We can point our finger and make up excuses, we can invent arguments and do anything else we want, but the key to the closet jingles in our pocket until we settle matters right. Proverbs 28:13 says,

> He who conceals his sins does not prosper, but whoever confesses and renounces them finds mercy.

In a day of permissive drop-out, cop-out, rip-off and let-yourself-go, we need to learn the foundational principle of all mental, social and spiritual health. We need to learn to confess and forsake our sins—not our excuses—in order to experience forgiveness.

STEP 27

Collapse in the Christian Life

Only four chapters in the Bible remain silent about sin and its dangers—the first two and the last two. Since Adam and Eve found themselves naked under the Tree of Knowledge of Good and Evil, sin has been common to all the human race.

The apostle John spells this out clearly: 'If we claim to be without sin, we deceive ourselves and the truth is not in us' (1 John 1:8). The deadliest sin is assuming we have no sin. None of us is free from the possibility of committing evil. Until we enjoy fruit from the Tree of Life in glory some day, we must admit our vulnerability.

William Wilberforce, the politician and reformer, said: 'There is no shortcut to holiness. It must be the business of (our) whole lives.' We can't be holy in a hurry.

'If you're saying some sin could never get you,' Dr Howard Hendricks writes, 'you're about to step on a spiritual banana peel.' Assuming invincibility is never a fail-safe security.

You and I both know of Christian leaders and laymen who have 'suddenly' fallen into sin. Everything seems to be going well for them—then they leave their wife for another woman...they attempt suicide...they become alcoholic. How does this happen? Dr George Sweeting comments, 'Collapse in the Christian life is rarely a blow-out—it's usually a slow leak.'

Our spiritual life is punctured and in danger of collapse whenever we lose sight of who God is. To the degree that we do not know God, we sin. Sin is man's declaration of independence. The first step away from God is ceasing to appreciate who God is and failing to thank him for his person and work in our lives. Unthankfulness and other forms of disobedience—whether in deed, thought or desire—produce certain results. When we sin, the Holy Spirit is grieved, Satan gains a foothold, we lose our joy in Christ, we find ourselves separated from God and others, we become a stumbling block to weaker brothers and we cause untold sorrow and grief.

Take a spiritual inventory of your own life. Consider: Who is God in my eyes? What is my relationship with him like? How often do I give thanks to him? Meditate on such passages as Psalm 34, Psalm 63:1–8 and 1 Thessalonians 5:16–24. Determine ways to apply these passages to your own life.

What comes to mind when you think about God is the most important thing about you. What comes from your lips throughout the day indicates whether or not you see and appreciate his sovereignty, grace and other attributes of divinity.

Is the Lord speaking to your heart? How is your relationship with him? Confess any known sins to God, my friend, and (like Paul) decide by God's enabling to live a victorious Christian life (1 Corinthians 9:24–27; Galatians 2:20). Speak forth the praises of the Lord you love and faithfully obey him.

Collapse in the Christian life never needs to happen.

STEP 28

God's Forgiveness

During World War II Hans Rookmaaker became active in the Dutch Resistance. Eventually, he was captured by the Germans and sent to a Nazi concentration camp where he began to read the Bible.

As he studied God's word, he discovered for himself that at the heart of God is the desire to forgive our sins. He gladly committed his life to Christ and revelled in his new-found joy and freedom.

When Rookmaaker was released from prison at the end of the war he immediately joined a church. But instead of being in fellowship with the free, he was surprised to find many Christians still in bondage to sin. They were not experiencing God's forgiveness.

On the other hand, a character in a play by Voltaire died muttering, 'C'est son métier' (God will forgive—that's his job). Forgiveness cannot be presupposed like that, but God never meant us to live in bondage.

The Bible teaches that confession is prerequisite to God's forgiveness—whether for initial salvation or daily fellowship. This confession involves repentance and restitution. Confession without repentance constitutes fraud. In Proverbs 28:13 we read,

> He who conceals his sins does not prosper, but whoever confesses and renounces them finds mercy.

Confession also involves restitution at times (Exodus

15). Usually this is the forgotten aspect of confession. our sin deprived someone of something that was ully theirs (whether goods or money or an honest amount of work), we must not only apologize to the offended person, but also seek to repay them.

The beauty of Scripture is its good news that God freely forgives those who properly confess their sins. Manasseh was one of the most wicked men to serve as king of Judah. He overturned Hezekiah's reforms and served false gods with more zeal than the nations God had destroyed before the Israelites (2 Chronicles 33:1–9). But after being captured by the Assyrians, Manasseh greatly humbled himself before the Lord—who forgave him! If God could forgive such a wicked and pagan king who humbled himself before the Lord, surely he will forgive us when we truly confess our sins and repent. Confession is humbling, but

> if we confess our sins, he is faithful and just and will forgive us our sins and purify us from all unrighteousness (1 John 1:9).

Learn this verse and claim it—often.

Here is another good verse to add to your Scripture memorization list: *'Their sins and lawless acts I will remember no more'* (Hebrews 10:17). How remarkable it is that the omniscient God promises not only to forgive our sins, but also to forget them forever!

'What better can we do,' Milton asks in *Paradise Lost*, 'than prostrate fall before him reverent; and there confess humbly our faults, and pardon beg; with tears watering the ground, and with our sighs the air frequenting, sent from hearts contrite, in sign of sorrow unfeigned, and humiliation meek?'

STEP 29

Perpetual Commotion

During the seventeenth century the Marquis of Worcester found himself imprisoned in the Tower of London. Being a clever gentleman, he built a curious contraption and asked an audience with the King.

In the King's presence he revealed his invention: a self-turning wheel. His Majesty was so impressed that he released his prisoner. Little did he suspect at the time that the Marquis had simply *simulated* a perpetual motion machine.

For at least 1,500 years various individuals have tried to design and build the world's first device that never stops moving. During the golden age of perpetual motion in England (from about 1850 to the turn of the century), nearly 600 patents for such devices were granted. The contraptions certainly look impressive on paper. But when built they never work! Recent perpetual motionists refuse to concede that it is impossible to break the laws of thermodynamics. Their perpetual commotion only succeeds in redesigning machines that were proven failures generations ago.

Similarly, men and women today ignore the clear statements of Scripture in their attempts to achieve the impossible. Futilely they seek to obtain eternal life and favour with God by their good deeds. Salvation, however, is not granted on the merits of our attainment, but on Christ's perfect atonement for our sins by his death on the cross. Only by committing our lives to him can we receive the assurance of sins forgiven and life eternal.

Salvation by works is a type of perpetual motion. It will

never work. In Romans 3:23 we read, 'All have sinned and fall short of the glory of God.' No matter how hard we try, we can't measure up to the perfect standard God requires before anyone can enter his presence. Thus, salvation can never be on the basis of what we do, but only on the basis of God's infinite mercy.

A mother once approached Napoleon seeking a pardon for her son. The emperor replied that the young man had committed a certain offence twice and justice demanded death.

'But I don't ask for justice,' the mother explained. 'I plead for mercy.'

'But your son does not deserve mercy,' Napoleon replied.

'Sir,' the woman cried, 'it would not be mercy if he deserved it, and mercy is all I ask for.'

'Well then,' the emperor said, 'I will have mercy.' And he spared her son.

Christians are not those who earn God's favour by their intrinsic goodness. They are merely recipients of God's mercy. God saves us, we read in Titus 3:5, 'not because of righteous things we had done, but because of his mercy.' Thankfully, we need but ask once to receive his gift of salvation freely.

Just as salvation is not attained by what we do, so it is not maintained by our good works. Our salvation rests on the sure promises of God. Christ himself has gone on record as saying,

> I tell you the truth, whoever hears my word and believes him who sent me has eternal life and will not be condemned; he has crossed over from death to life (John 5:24).

All the perpetual commotion in the world cannot save an individual, no matter how ingenious his efforts may appear. And all the uproar in hell cannot change the certainty of God's salvation once we receive it.

STEP 30

Letting Go of Guilt

As Christians we rejoice that our salvation is secure in Christ and we know that our sins are forever washed away by his blood. We marvel at God's infinite mercy to forgive us even though we don't deserve it. But often we won't forgive ourselves!

Yes, we know that 'as far as the east is from the west, so far has he removed our transgressions from us' (Psalm 103:12). But from sunrise to sunset we needlessly carry the heavy burden of guilt.

For some reason we feel compelled to carry these heavy burdens, even though God never designed us that way. We need to learn to let go of our guilt.

Sometimes our burden of guilt is nothing more than false condemnation. When I was a youth, my mother absolutely believed the bottom of the cinema would open up and drop me straight into the fire of hell if I ever went to see a film, regardless of its message. I felt bad even at walking past a cinema. Now *that* was false guilt.

Paul Tournier, the respected psychologist, has said, 'False guilt comes as a result of judgements and suggestions of men.' People sometimes seek to control or manipulate us by inventing rules or regulations that the Bible never mentions. We need to carefully and prayerfully identify such false guilt and let go of it.

On other occasions we carry heavy burdens of guilt because we don't deal with it properly. There are at least three inappropriate responses to true guilt.

we can *repress* our guilt. We try to cover it up and
existence. We focus on our insignificant faults
of acknowledging our real guilt. As a result, we
lose our peace and often suffer physically as well.

Second, we can *regret* our 'mistake'. But saying 'I'm
sorry' fails to acknowledge the seriousness of our sin and
our responsibility.

Third, we can have *remorse* for our sin. 'I'll never do it
again,' we promise. Judas felt remorse after betraying
Christ (Matthew 27:3–4). But he fell one step short of
what the Bible calls repentance.

Repentance is the biblical, correct response to guilt.
The moment we committed our life to Christ, our sins—
past, present and future—were forgiven. God's righteousness was satisfied. But now as children of God we must
maintain fellowship. This necessitates confessing our sins
to our heavenly Father as we become aware of them.

C. S. Lewis said that true guilt is an inner alarm system
which reveals sin in our lives and shows our loss of fellowship with God. The Holy Spirit uses guilt to prompt us to
turn *from* our sin and back *to* the Father.

Once we let go of false guilt and properly deal with our
sins, we are free from the burden of guilt. Isaiah 55:6–7
gives us this assurance:

> Seek the Lord while he may be found;
>   call on him while he is near.
> Let the wicked forsake his way
>   and the evil man his thoughts.
> Let him turn to the Lord, and he will have mercy on him,
>   and to our God, for he will freely pardon.

Let go of your burdens and turn to God today.

STEP 31

Forgive and Forget

My friend, has anyone ever offended you? Has your spouse been unfaithful? Have your children disappointed you? Has someone cheated you in business? How we respond to the difficult experiences of life directly affects our spiritual well-being.

My father died when I was only ten years old. He left us quite a bit of property and some money. But his four brothers squandered everything we had. In three years my family was living in poverty and debt. When I was older and really understood what they had done, I urged my mother to take revenge on them, to get a lawyer to take them to court and let them have it. The older I got, the more bitter I became.

But the Bible says,

> Do not take revenge, my friends, but leave room for God's wrath, for it is written: "It is mine to avenge; I will repay," says the Lord (Romans 12:19).

He is the one who measures out justice. He wants to handle such judgement for us—perhaps now, certainly ultimately. My mother always quoted verses like Romans 12:19. She completely forgave my uncles for what they did. It took us twenty years to finish paying our debts. But she refused to become bitter. She forgot what they had done. Consequently, God gave her a freedom of spirit and opportunities to serve him. I experienced that same freedom and fruitfulness years later when I, too, finally forgave my uncles.

How deeply have you been hurt? Have you become bitter or unforgiving in your attitude?

I would like to remind you of the story of Joseph. I encourage you to read the account of his life in Genesis 37–50. It is an exciting portion of Scripture! This passage shows us many valuable lessons on the importance of forgiving and forgetting. The Bible gives us many reasons why Joseph could have been a very bitter man. His brothers hated him and sold him into slavery. His master's wife falsely accused him of a serious crime and had him thrown into an Egyptian prison. A government official promised to help him yet left him there to rot. Despite all these things, Joseph did not allow any root of bitterness to take hold in his life (compare Hebrews 12:15).

Many lives in Britain are spoiled by bitterness and a lack of forgiveness. People go through physical and emotional breakdowns because they refuse to forgive others. The longer we carry a grudge, the heavier it becomes. We cannot afford to harbour bitterness in our soul. It will destroy us. The Bible says,

> Bear with each other and forgive whatever grievances you may have against one another. Forgive as the Lord forgave you (Colossians 3:13).

After entering into the experience of forgiving someone, forgetfulness is vital. Joseph called his first-born son Manasseh, 'It is because God has made me forget all my trouble and all my father's household' (Genesis 41:51). Joseph not only forgave his brothers, but he forgot the evil deeds they had committed against him.

Like Joseph, keep short accounts with God and men. Don't lock bitterness and guilt within the closet of your soul. Forgive and forget. This is a secret for spiritual health.

STEP 32

Doing What Our Father Says

More than ninety people conducted an all-night search in early 1983 for Dominic DeCarlo, an eight-year-old boy lost on a snowy mountain slope. Dominic, who had been on a skiing trip with his father, Ray, had apparently ridden on a new lift and skied off the run without realizing it.

As each hour passed, the search party and the boy's family became more and more concerned for his health and safety. By dawn they had found no trace of the young boy. Two helicopters joined the search, and within 15 minutes had spotted ski tracks. A ground team followed the tracks, which changed to small footprints. The footprints led to a tree where they found the boy at last.

'He's in super shape,' announced Sgt Terry Silbaugh, area search and rescue co-ordinator, to the anxious family and press. 'In fact, he's in better shape than we are right now.' A hospital spokeswoman said the boy was in fine condition and wasn't even admitted.

Sgt Silbaugh explained why the boy did so well despite spending a night in the freezing elements: his father had enough forethought to warn the boy what to do if he became lost, and his son had enough trust to do exactly what his father said. Dominic protected himself from possible frostbite and hypothermia by snuggling up to a tree and covering himself with branches. As a young child, he never would have thought of doing that on his own. He was simply obeying his wise and loving father.

Dominic reminds me of what we should do as children of our loving and infinitely wise heavenly Father. We are not to walk any more according to the course of this world which is passing away. Instead, we are to walk in obedience to the Lord's commands. After all, he knows what is best for us. That's one of the reasons I believe the Bible is so relevant for us today. The apostle Peter tells us:

> As obedient children, do not conform to the evil desires you had when you lived in ignorance. But just as he who called you is holy, so be holy in all you do; for it is written: "Be holy, because I am holy" (1 Peter 1:14–16).

In Christ we enjoy a holy standing before God. In 2 Corinthians 5:21 we discover that

> God made him who had no sin to be sin for us, so that in him we might become the righteousness of God.

But our actual *state* here on earth is sometimes a different story.

Because our Father is holy, and because in Christ we have a holy standing, we are exhorted in Scripture to be holy in all we do. Thus, every time we sin, we forget who we are and why we are alive. We forget what is truly best for us. Yes, we can find forgiveness from the Father when we sin (1 John 2:1–2). But sin is not to be the trademark of our lives.

In a world full of deceptive detours and confusing paths, let's trust our Father and do exactly what he has said.

STEP 33

God's Fences for Freedom

Do God's commandments excite you? Do you enjoy studying them—and obeying them? When was the last time, for example, that you seriously contemplated the Ten Commandments?

'Now, Luis,' you say, 'who gets excited about the Ten Commandments today?'

When I was growing up in Argentina, God's commandments—especially the Ten Commandments—were taught in such a legalistic way that I avoided any serious study of them until after I had finished my biblical studies in the United States. I discovered then how little has ever been written about them.

Our sinful nature causes us to corrupt that which is beautiful. We turn God's moral law, which the apostle Paul called 'holy, righteous and good' (Romans 7:12), into oppressive legalism. Perhaps that's why we frown at the mere mention of the Ten Commandments.

'They remind me of my grandmother who had a fit if I ever wanted to play outside on Sundays,' some will admit.

'Thinking of the Commandments reminds me of my father who refused to read the Sunday newspaper.'

The words of God should not elicit such reactions. Let's return to God's moral law and shake off the chains of well-intending, sincere, but sinful human beings who have twisted the beauty of God's commandments.

When the Lord gave Israel the Ten Commandments he said:

Listen, O Israel! I brought you out of bondage, not to create another bondage for you, but to liberate you. And if you remain within the boundaries that I am about to give you then you will be free. You'll have plenty of room to manoeuvre. So enjoy all that I have given to you.

God's statement includes a warning:

As long as you stay within the fence you will be free, but once you try to stretch the boundaries or jump over the fence, you will be in bondage once again.

I am convinced that this is the way God intends us to view his commandments. The apostle John reminds us, 'His commands are not burdensome' (1 John 5:3). They are life!

Now obviously we are not to try to live up to the Ten Commandments for our salvation. We are all sinners (Romans 3:23) in need of a Saviour, Jesus Christ (Romans 5:8). Both the Bible and experience teach us that we couldn't keep the Ten Commandments even if we tried (Romans 7:1–8:4).

The purpose of God's commandments is not to provide salvation, but rather to lay a foundation for us—a foundation to build more and more of the characteristics of Jesus Christ who indwells us after we receive him (Galatians 2:20; 3:19–29).

Spend some time meditating on God's commandments. Start with the Ten Commandments in Exodus 20:1–17. As you study and pray answer these questions. First, what does each commandment reveal about the character of God? Second, what does each commandment liberate me from? Third, how does each commandment protect me? Finally, if love is the fulfilment of the law (Galatians 5:14), then what does each of the commandments reveal about love?

I believe once you answer these four questions, you will never look at God's commandments with a negative attitude again. As you look at them with the proper perspective, I think you will uncover at least four principles which will enhance your understanding of our infinitely wise and loving heavenly Father.

STEP 34

Meeting God within His Fences

In the last chapter we considered how we often turn God's commandments into oppressive legalism, but that God meant them to liberate us!

In my personal study of the Ten Commandments, I have learned four principles which have enhanced my own understanding of our heavenly Father's infinite wisdom and love.

1. God's commandments reveal his character

To me, the most exciting aspect of the Ten Commandments is that they reveal God's character. See how the list from your study compares with mine. We worship a God who is possessive (Exodus 20:3); jealous, in that he hates idolatry (20:4–6); holy and honourable, deserving respect (20:7); desirous that we preserve the sanctity of worship and learn to rest in him (20:8–11); wants to protect the family (20:12); reveres life (20:13); desires godly offspring, sexual purity and holy people (20:14); delights in giving gifts and not having them taken away (20:15); can be trusted 100 per cent (20:16); looks on the inner reality of each heart (20:17).

How do our lists compare? Aren't the Ten Commandments a great place to start a study on holiness and the character of God?

2. God's commandments show genuine liberation

Today's society generates a tremendous sense of bondage. People constantly talk about their need to break away, go out on their own and be free. Ironically, people believe that breaking God's moral law is the road to liberation. Yet all they experience is further enslavement. Only God's moral law reveals genuine liberation. This seems especially true within dating and marital relationships.

3. God's commandments provide complete protection

After reading the Ten Commandments carefully, can you see how God designed them to protect us socially, politically, economically and physically? And most of all do you see how they protect us spiritually from our adversary, the devil, who would like nothing better than to destroy us (1 Peter 5:8)?

One of the ways Satan attacks us is by tempting us to climb over one of God's fences. But we can have victory because Christ dwells in us (1 John 4:4).

4. God's commandments reveal true love

Did you read through the Ten Commandments to learn what each command reveals about love? Let's compare lists again.

I reveal my love for the Father by giving him his unique and proper supreme place in my life (Exodus 20:3); by not attributing characteristics to him that are not revealed in Scripture (20:4–6); by setting aside a day each week for honouring God and worshipping with my family and the family of God (20:8–11); by honouring my parents which ultimately reveals God's love toward us in our older years, and his desire that we have happy homes (20:12); by respecting life and doing unto others as we would have them do unto us (20:13); by not playing games with our sexuality (20:14); by delighting in being generous for the Lord (20:15); by being trustworthy and God-honouring in our speech (20:16); by being content, holy and sanctified through the power of the Holy Spirit who dwells in us (20:17).

God's commandments also reveal his vast love for us.

81

Because we could never measure up to his glory and holiness, he provided us with a Saviour—his Son, Jesus Christ. When we repent, seek forgiveness and commit ourselves to Christ, he comes to live in us. It is only then that we can truly call the loving and wise Lord 'our Father who is in heaven'.

STEP 35

Out of Bounds

The boundary line seemed old and irrelevant. Sarah tapped the line with her foot, wondering what would happen if she crossed it. At last, at the persuasion of her boyfriend, Andy, she stepped over.

Several weeks later, 16-year-old Sarah discovered she was pregnant. 'I'll never forget the panic,' she admits. 'Andy was in Cyprus and I was living at home with my Dad...I just didn't know where to turn.'

Andy came back from Cyprus and the two teenagers were married. But Sarah's problems are far from solved. Loneliness, financial pressures and regret plague her.

'I hope Andy and I will stay together, though being a soldier he's away a lot, and I get bored being stuck at home all day,' Sarah confesses. 'So maybe one day we'll split up. The thing is you have to try so hard to make marriage work and divorce is so easy.'

God's standard of sexual purity before marriage seemed out of date to Sarah. She didn't realize God had wisely and lovingly established that boundary for her own protection. Now she is suffering the consequences of her disobedience.

What are the consequences of going out of bounds sexually, whether single or married? Ask King David. In Psalm 38 he describes the effects of his personal sin— apparently that of committing adultery with Bathsheba. David experienced the agony of spiritual discipline (verses 1–2), physical torment (verses 3–10), social isolation (verses 11–16) and emotional anxiety (verses 17–22). Quite a high price to pay for a moment of uncontrolled passion, wouldn't you say?

God's standards for purity in interpersonal relationships are far from out of date, even though they contradict today's cultural norms. Young people today say premarital sex is okay—94 percent forfeit their virginity by the age of 21, as I mentioned in Step 23. But God says:

> Flee from sexual immorality. All other sins a man commits are outside his body, but he who sins sexually sins against his own body. Do you not know that your body is a temple of the Holy Spirit, who is in you, whom you have received from God? You are not your own; you were bought at a price. Therefore honour God with your body (1 Corinthians 6:18–20).

Christian young people struggle with the same temptations unbelieving peers face. The devil often uses an unhealthy Christian/non-Christian dating relationship to cause a believer to stumble. The Lord warns us:

> Do not be yoked together with unbelievers. For what do righteousness and wickedness have in common? Or what fellowship can light have with darkness? What harmony is there between Christ and Belial? What does a believer have in common with an unbeliever? What agreement is there between the temple of God and idols? For we are the temple of the living God (2 Corinthians 6:14–16).

Especially if you're single, take the verses above to heart. Develop biblical convictions for dating and relating to those of the opposite sex. Then enjoy the satisfaction that comes from a Christ-centred relationship kept within his wise and loving boundaries.

STEP 36

Dating and Courtship

On the way to a class party one day, I noticed several girls. 'Are you going to the party?' I asked. They all said yes, and for some reason I asked òne of them, 'Can I walk you over?'

She said, 'Sure.' It was no big deal. We weren't even together at the party, but I started becoming interested in this young woman. Pat was fun and talkative. She seemed mature and intelligent, she knew how to dress well, and in conversation I discovered that she was very spiritually sensitive.

I don't know what Pat thought of me at first—she still won't tell me—but I began looking for her on campus. In fact, my window overlooked a walkway to the cafeteria, and I watched for her every morning and then 'just happened' to pop out of the door when she came by.

I had never studied much in the library before, but when I found out Pat usually did her homework there, that's where I could be found, too. I kept one eye on my book and the other on her. Pat finally caught on that I was interested in her, and we saw a lot of each other. At first there was nothing serious between us, but I certainly hoped there would be!

I'll be the first to admit I made mistakes while I dated and courted Pat. But let me share three or four key words with you from my experience that will help you to develop a quality relationship with someone of the opposite sex.

The first word is *Courtesy*. Courtesy is a sign of genuine

love. Now by love I don't mean matrimonial love, but the type of love that comes from God. In 1 Corinthians 13:5, we read that love is not rude or self-seeking. Instead, love gives to the other person without planning to get something else in return.

Someone has said, 'Good habits are made of little sacrifices.' I like that. The habit of courtesy consists of little and insignificant sacrifices which show our interest in the other person. Discover what your special friend enjoys. Does she like flowers? Surprise her with a small bouquet of her favourite type. Show thoughtfulness and respect as you spend time together getting to know each other.

Another important word to remember is *Conversation*. Paul tells us in Colossians 4:6, 'Let your conversation be always full of grace.' Nothing is better for a good friendship than positive and uplifting talks. I still remember the many discussions Pat and I enjoyed the year before we were married.

Often relationships between a fellow and girl focus—even depend—on showing physical affection. But as Solomon wrote, there is a time to embrace, and a time to refrain (Ecclesiastes 3:5). Focus instead on learning more about each other's interests, family, friends, dreams, priorities, walk with the Lord. Ask lots of questions—*and listen!* The best conversation is the one you initiate with questions.

In the next step I want to share two more key words with you about dating and courting. Until you read it, if you are dating or engaged, talk with your special friend about making courtesy and conversation part of your relationship.

STEP 37

More about Dating and Courtship

There were only a few more days before the Christmas break, and I was anxious for it to come. I would be visiting friends, but mostly I was weary of my courses. My studies at Multnomah School of the Bible had been exciting but intense.

But deep in my heart I almost didn't want the break to come. I was becoming more interested in Pat all the time, and when I learned she was going away over the holidays and had a few calls to make, I worried that one of those calls might be to see an old boyfriend.

So I let Pat know how I felt about her. It wasn't anything dramatic or romantic, just my usual, straight-out Latin style. I wanted her to know that she was special to me, that I cared about her a great deal, and that I hoped we could spend a lot more time together after the holidays.

I really missed her over Christmas and was anxious to get back to school. The second term was exciting, although my grades dropped a bit. Pat can take some of the credit for that. I spent all the time with her that I could.

Two words characterized our relationship during this period of courtship. One word is *Knowledge*. As Pat and I conversed and spent time together, I became an expert on her. I started to discover not only what she thought, but why she felt the way she did. It's true that you can only love someone to the degree that you know him or her.

'Falling in love' with someone the first time you meet them may sound romantic, but a true love relationship won't last long on first impressions. Be careful that you don't develop an idealistic image of the other person based on those impressions—you'll be disappointed sooner or later. Honesty and openness are vital right from the start. Grow in love as you deepen your understanding and appreciation for the other person.

The other word that describes our relationships is *Spirituality*. Pat's personality, intelligence and attractive appearance caught my eye when I first met her, certainly. But as we grew to know each other better, I discovered her deep commitment to Christ and desire to follow his will. And, to my mind, that was so important. At last I knew I wanted to spend the rest of my life serving the Lord together with Pat.

By the Valentine's Day banquet that year we were unofficially engaged. I didn't exactly ask her to marry me, though. In my typical romantic fashion, as we walked under an umbrella in the Portland rain, I asked her if she would return to South America with me. She knew what that entailed. And I knew what her 'yes' meant, too. We were married several months later.

As Christians, we should not only marry someone who is a Christian (1 Corinthians 7:39), but someone who is a *growing* Christian. Someone whose life is marked by spirituality. Ask yourself these questions: 'Does the person I love challenge me to grow closer to the Lord? Or do I find he/she sometimes hinders my spiritual growth?'

Decide before God to date and marry only someone with whom you could seek the kingdom of God for a lifetime. Nothing could be more exciting or thrilling!

STEP 38

Two Shall Become One

Some marriages may be made in heaven, but many of the details have to be worked out here on earth. Unfortunately, many couples enter into an intimate relationship with little or no thought about how such a relationship is designed to work.

'I only married to get away from home, to get a house of my own and be independent,' admits Jane, a young woman from Yorkshire. 'My parents tried to talk me out of it but you always think you know better.'

Jane thought she was breaking from her parents. In reality, her marriage was only a contest to prove she knew best. She failed to develop a close bond with her husband, however, and 'after six months I knew it was a mistake— even before my baby was born.' Shortly afterward her marriage dissolved.

The names change, the circumstances vary, but the tragedy remains the same: One in three marriages in Britain eventually ends in divorce. A well-known Christian leader made this observation: 'All of my counselling in marriage and family problems can be categorized on the basis of these three situations: failure to truly leave the parents; failure to cleave to the one partner; or failure to develop a unified relationship.'

Leave. Cleave. Unify. Moses, the Lord Jesus Christ and later the Apostle Paul all used these same three concepts to describe how God designed marriage to work. 'For this reason a man will leave his father and mother and be united to his wife, and the two will become one flesh' (Mark 10:7–8).

Marriage involves leaving our parents and clinging to our spouse. It is a total, intimate, exclusive union between a man and his wife. But that's not all! Christian marriage is really a triangle: a man, a woman, and Christ. My wife, Pat, committed her life to Christ at the age of eight. Christ came into my heart at the age of twelve. When we joined our lives together, we did so in the presence of the Lord. He is the third party in our marriage. He is the one who keeps us together and draws us closer to one another as we seek to draw closer to him.

God has designed man and woman to complement each other in the marital relationship—spiritually, intellectually, emotionally, socially and physically. Intimacy starts with spiritual oneness in Christ, and eventually knits a couple together in every area of life. This takes time and commitment. But the rewards of such intimacy and oneness are fantastic!

'But Luis,' you say, 'my spouse and I aren't experiencing that oneness in our marriage. In fact, sometimes I feel we don't even know each other. Often we disagree with each other or just go our separate ways. What should we do?'

When marital problems surface, don't run away from God. Instead, run to him. Come to Christ. Lay the problem at his feet with your spouse. Gather your spouse in your arms by your bedside. Open up your Bible, kneel together, read a passage and talk about what it says. See what God's word has to say about your situation. Then share prayer requests and talk to God about them together. By doing this you will learn more about your spouse and God will show you how two can become one—and grow yet closer every day.

STEP 39

God's Blueprint for Happy Homes

No nation is stronger than its homes. One Chinese proverb says, 'If there is harmony in the home, there will be order in the nation.' The family unit is the basic foundation on which human society is built. The fragmentation of our families, however, will prove to be the destruction of our civilization.

Four prevalent attitudes attack our homes from every side. *Secularism* advocates, 'Grab with all the gusto you can because you only go around once in life!' *Materialism* says, 'Get more, buy more, build more!' *Sensualism* joins in by bombarding us with immorality and perversion through the media. *Humanism* concludes, 'Glory to man in the highest—we don't need God.'

No matter what these philosophies claim, they have managed only to erode the family unit. Why? Because they oppose God's blueprint for happy homes. After all, he invented the family. And he has given us his blueprint in the Bible so that we can discover what he says to spouses, parents and children.

First of all, the Bible teaches us that we are to rest in each other's strength. Ephesians 5:21 says, 'Submit to one another out of reverence for Christ.' Because Christ is the Lord of our family, we should treat each other with respect as he has instructed. I can't have my way all the time, nor can my wife or children. We must seek to do things God's way.

Submission is necessary for order and stability. Otherwise, everyone tries to do his own thing without any accountability. One hit song boasts, 'I did it my way!' Go ahead and do it your way—and see how many people you hurt in the process, including yourself.

Sometimes we have this idea that the man can't show any weaknesses. He must wear a mask to cover up his true feelings. But that's false! The Bible teaches that the husband is to rely on his wife and she is to rest in him as the spiritual leader of their home.

That doesn't mean either is inferior. Men and women are equal in God's eyes. Paul makes this clear when he says, 'There is neither...male nor female, for you are all one in Christ Jesus' (Galatians 3:28).

Within the home, God knows the family best functions with a leader. That's why he has designated the man to take that responsibility and exercise it with love. Sometimes my wife, Pat, is better at making rational decisions than I am. Yet she rests upon me to make the final choices that must be made in our home. But in turn, I often rely on her counsel and advice. We complement and support each other.

As children see their parents' mutual submission to one another, they more easily respect and obey their father and mother (Ephesians 6:1–3), especially if they are disciplined in love for their own good (Hebrews 12:5–11).

God's blueprint for happy homes *does* make a difference! I encourage you to read the Bible and pray as a family each day to learn more about his blueprint for your home.

STEP 40

Family Worship

Some of the most important things you and I will ever say and do will be at home. That's where life's most crucial curriculum is taught to our children. On the average, our children spend one per cent of their time in church, 16 per cent in school, and the remaining 83 per cent in and around the home.

Columbia University in New York spent approximately £170,000 on a research project only to discover a biblical truth: there is no second force in a child's life compared to the impact of his home.

The influence of a godly parent cannot be over-estimated. Unless our children see the difference Christ makes in our lives and hear the Gospel clearly presented, they will almost invariably reject Christianity.

God has no grandchildren. I discovered that as a boy. My parents both loved and served the Lord Jesus Christ, but the day came when I had to decide to commit my life to him, too.

God has designed the home as the place where his word is to be taught, lived, and passed on from generation to generation.

Deuteronomy 6:6–7 says:

> These commandments that I give you today are to be upon your hearts. Impress them on your children. Talk about them when you sit at home and when you walk along the road, when you lie down and when you get up.

Someone has said: 'Train up a child in the way he should go, and walk there every once in awhile yourself.' As our children rub shoulders with us around the table and during other times in the day, they are noticing every attitude we convey and every word we say—and carefully imitating us. Can you honestly say to your children, without embarrassment, 'Follow my example, as I follow the example of Christ' (1 Corinthians 11:1)?

One of the most important ways parents communicate their faith to their children is to lead them in family worship. Time for Bible study and prayer should be a natural, enjoyable and daily part of your family life. Involve your children in reading a short passage of Scripture and discussing what it means. Seek to be creative— it's a 'sin' to bore someone when you're teaching the Bible.

Prayer is another important aspect of family worship that should extend to every part of the day—before school, meals and bedtime. Teach your children to thank God for his protection and goodness, confess their sins, and pray for relatives and friends.

We have a stewardship with every child God gives us. Generally, we have them in our home for only a short time before they leave and establish their own families.

We need to pray that God will 'teach us to number our days aright' (Psalm 90:12). 'Life is a short and fevered rehearsal for a concert we cannot stay to give,' A. W. Tozer wrote. Because our time is so limited, we must decide what we will and will not do in order to best bring our children up in the 'training and instruction of the Lord' (Ephesians 6:4).

Make it a priority to say and do those things that will teach your children life's most important lessons. Use family worship as a means to integrate Christianity into every aspect of your home.

STEP 41

Who Needs the Church?

'I don't go to any church or religious meetings now,' one woman acknowledged. 'My religion is being with God. I don't need any help with that.' A college student added:

> The church is beyond hypocrisy for me. I see it as dull, irrelevant, afraid of life, betraying God, and trying to save its own skin. There are some great individual people inside it, but they represent about one-half of one per cent of the total membership. So the church for me is dead. God is very much alive, but God doesn't need the church.

Who needs the church, anyway? Britain set aside an entire year to reflect on her deep spiritual roots in a celebration called 'Christian Heritage'. But how Christian is Britain today? A BBC reporter once asked me why I was wasting my time trying to evangelize a post-Christian society. 'Aren't you just flogging a dead horse?' he wondered out loud.

'There is no such thing as a post-Christian society,' I replied. 'One generation may reject the Gospel for itself, but it can't reject it for future generations. And furthermore,' I gladly added, 'Jesus Christ specializes in raising the dead.'

A miracle tantamount to resurrection is needed to reverse the retrenchment of the British church. This downward trend has continued almost unabated for more than half a century. In 1984 it was reckoned that church members form 17% of the adult population in the UK.

And the figure is dropping!

So, who needs the church today? I believe we all need the church. We need to meet together as groups of believers to devote ourselves to 'teaching and to the fellowship, to the breaking of bread and to prayer' (Acts 2:42).

The church, after all, is not a building or a denomination. It is *people*. And I believe there is a movement of God today among many Christians throughout this land that I love so much.

Are you already a member of a local church? Pray that God will move in a mighty way to revive the churches in Britain.

If you have become discouraged about the church, remember what the Scripture says:

> Let us not give up meeting together, as some are in the habit of doing, but let us encourage one another—and all the more as you see the Day approaching' (Hebrews 10:25).

Seek fellowship with a church that preaches—and practises—God's word. Too many pastors today are trying to feed their congregations social pabulum instead of truth. No wonder people are leaving the church dissatisfied!

The Lord wants to bless Britain in a marvellous and superlative way. And he's going to do it, I believe, as each member of the Body of Christ wakes up to his responsibilities to minister within his church and evangelize those who still need to hear the voice of God. Won't you join me in praying and working toward that end?

STEP 42

Any Old Bush Will Do

I've heard it said that whether this is the best of times or the worst of times, it's the only time we've got. This is a good reminder for Christians. This is our moment in history. We must serve the Lord daily during the time that we do have. But how can we serve? How can we be victorious for Christ during our lifetime? What characterizes a genuine and successful Christian worker?

Many Christians believe that if they work hard enough and pray long enough, then they'll be victorious. That's the essence of legalism. Sincere as a legalist may be, if he is relying on himself then he is heading for a terrible fall. This was the case with Moses when he killed the Egyptian who had been beating a Hebrew slave. He was sincere in his intentions, but he was relying on his own power, the weapons of the flesh.

It was also my situation when I came to the United States in 1961 to further my biblical studies. I had big dreams that I wanted to see quickly accomplished. My impatience led me to rely on my own power, not the Lord's.

During one of the last chapel services at college before our break, our speaker was Major Ian Thomas, founder of the Torchbearers in England. Major Thomas' theme was, 'Any old bush will do, as long as God is in the bush.'

He pointed out that it took Moses 40 years in the wilderness to get the point that he was nothing. God was trying to tell Moses, 'I don't need a pretty bush or an educated bush or an eloquent bush. Any old bush will do, as long as I am in the bush. If I am going to use you, *I* am going to use you. It will not be you doing something for me, but me doing something through you.'

Major Thomas suggested that the bush in the desert was likely a dry bunch of ugly little sticks that had hardly developed, yet Moses had to take off his shoes. Why? Because this was holy ground. Why? Because God was in the bush!

I was like that bush. I could do nothing for God. All my reading, studying, asking questions and trying to model myself on others was worthless. Everything in my ministry was worthless, unless God was in me! No wonder I felt so frustrated. Only he could make something happen.

When Major Thomas closed with Galatians 2:20, it all came together.

> I have been crucified with Christ and I no longer live, but Christ lives in me. The life I live in the body, I live by faith in the Son of God, who loved me and gave himself for me.

I realized that the secret of being a successful Christian worker was depending on the indwelling, resurrected, almighty Lord Jesus, and not myself. God was finally in control of this bush! Our inner resource is God himself, because of our union with Jesus Christ (Colossians 2: 9–15). Out of this understanding comes a godly sense of self-worth.

I had tremendous peace because I realized I didn't have to struggle any more. How sad that I had wasted eight years of my life trying to do everything in my own power.

Perhaps that might be your situation today. Remember, we cannot work or earn our victories through any self-effort, any more than we can work for our salvation.

Although our days on earth are short, they can be the best of times for us. They can count for eternity if we will only come to the end of ourselves and say, 'Not I, but Christ living in me.'

STEP 43

Speak Well of God's Son

One cold, windy night two Christian youths headed toward the tavern district in their hometown of Glasgow, Scotland, with the 'preposterous' idea of holding an open-air Gospel meeting. The youths began singing hymns to gather a crowd. Their singing was tolerated, but whenever they stopped singing to share the saving message of Jesus Christ, they were mocked by the crowd with vulgar hoots and jeering howls.

Frederick S. Arnot and his friend were quite sincere about sharing their faith and the Gospel message with the drunks along the tavern row. Yet the crowd was determined not to let them talk. Finally, Arnot, with tears running down his face, acknowledged defeat. He and his friend turned to leave.

Suddenly, someone grabbed Arnot's shoulder. Startled, Arnot turned to find a tall, elderly man towering over him. The stranger smiled warmly and quietly said, 'Keep at it, laddie; God loves to hear men speak well of his Son.'

With that encouragement, the two Scottish lads squared their shoulders and returned to the tavern row. It wasn't long before the rowdy crowd began to pay attention to the message the boys wanted to share.

In 1881, several years after this incident, Arnot, influenced by the example set by David Livingstone, left his Scottish mission field and headed for Central Africa, where God used him in a great way to proclaim the Gospel.

God loves to hear men and women speak well of his Son. Yet how easy it is for us to become silent about our faith because of discouragement, lack of results or some other excuse. Do you speak well of God's Son? If not, what is your excuse?

Recently I read an honest and challenging article entitled 'Excuses'. In the article the author, seminary professor Norman L. Geisler, admits that even though he was in full-time Christian ministry for 18 years, he never witnessed for Christ. His excuses sound familiar, don't they?

1. I didn't have the gift of evangelism. It was obvious to me that someone like Billy Graham did, and it was equally obvious that I didn't.

2. I had the gift of teaching (Christians) and it's pretty hard to make converts from that group.

3. I didn't like...impersonal evangelism, so I would do 'friendship evangelism'. I wasn't going to cram the gospel down anybody's throat.

4. I came to the conclusion that if God is sovereign...then he can do it with or without me.

One day, however, a visiting speaker demolished Geisler's excuses by saying, 'I've been a missionary for years and I was never *called*...I was just *commanded* like the rest of you.' That statement startled Geisler and he became a fisher of men.

'Go into all the world and preach the good news to all creation' (Mark 16:15) wasn't a suggestion, but a command of the Lord Jesus Christ. Perhaps you were once eager like Arnot to witness for Christ, but somehow that zeal has faded. Remember that God loves to hear you speak well of his Son.

STEP 44

The Greatest Thrill

As a young man I was excited about preaching the Gospel of Jesus Christ at street meetings, children's meetings and rallies. I prayed and studied and preached, but I felt frustrated.

The day came when I decided I didn't have the gift of evangelism. It was obvious. No matter how zealously I preached, no one was coming to Christ. Nothing I did seemed to make a difference. I was inspired by the things I read and heard about Billy Graham's ministry, but I knew I didn't have whatever he had.

I gave God a deadline:

> If I don't see any converts through my preaching by the end of the year, I'm quitting.

Oh, I would still be an active Christian, but I would resign myself to simply teaching other believers.

The end of the year came and went. No converts. My mind was made up: I was through preaching. Now I was sure I didn't have the gift.

On Saturday morning, about four days into the new year, the small church I attended held a cottage meeting. I didn't feel like going, but I went anyway out of loyalty to the elders.

The fellow who was supposed to teach the Bible study failed to appear. So the man of the house said, 'Luis, you are going to have to say something.' I was completely unprepared.

I had been reading a book, however, by Graham called *The Secret of Happiness,* which is based on the Beatitudes. So I asked for a New Testament and read Matthew 5:1–12. Then I simply repeated whatever I remembered from Graham's book.

As I was commenting on the Beatitude, 'Blessed are the pure in heart, for they shall see God,' a lady suddenly stood up. She began to cry and said, 'My heart is not pure. How can I see God? Somebody tell me how I can get a pure heart.' How delightful it was to lead her to Jesus Christ!

I don't remember the woman's name, but I will never forget her words: 'Somebody tell me how I can get a pure heart.' Together we read the Bible, 'The blood of Jesus, his Son, purifies us from every sin' (1 John 1:7). Before the evening was over that woman found peace with God and she went home with a pure heart overflowing with joy.

When you win people to Jesus Christ it's the greatest joy. Your graduation is exciting. Your wedding day is exciting. Your first baby is exciting. But the most thrilling thing you can ever do is win someone to Christ. And, you know, it's contagious. Once you do it, you don't want to stop.

I challenge you to pray: 'Dear God, I want that experience. I want to know what it is to win someone to Jesus Christ.'

Corrie ten Boom, the Dutch evangelist who went to be with her Saviour recently, had a God-given desire to win others to Christ. I would like to share one of her poems with you:

When I enter that beautiful city
    And the saints all around me appear,
I hope that someone will tell me:
    'It was you who invited me here'.

Whatever our place in the Body of Christ, let's enlarge our vision to invite one more person into God's kingdom. After all, God doesn't have a plan A, a plan B, and a plan C for evangelizing the world. He only has one plan—and that's you and me.

STEP 45

A Vision for Evangelism

At the end of World War II, Robert Woodruff declared, 'In my generation it is my desire that everyone in the world have a taste of Coca-Cola.' Talk about vision! Today Coca-Cola is sold from the deserts of Africa to the interior of China. Why? Because Woodruff motivated his colleagues to reach their generation around the world for Coke.

How big is your vision? Have you ever dreamed about what God could do through you to help win the world in our generation to Jesus Christ? After all, the only generation that can reach our generation, Oswald Smith has said, is our generation.

Even though the Lord limited his own public ministry to the Palestine area, he came and lived and died for the whole world. After his resurrection, he commissioned his disciples to 'make disciples of *all* nations' (Matthew 28:19) and sent them first to Jerusalem, then to all Judea and Samaria, and ultimately to the ends of the earth (Acts 1:8).

The early church was hesitant to dream about how God would fulfil Christ's last commands. The apostle Paul challenged their complacency by devoting his life after his conversion to travelling and proclaiming Christ.

Paul explains his vision for evangelism in Romans 15. First, he could report, 'From Jerusalem all the way around to Illyricum, I have fully proclaimed the Gospel of Christ' (Romans 15:19). Even his enemies admitted Paul had saturated entire provinces with the gospel (Acts 19:26) and turned the world upside down (Acts 17:6).

Paul was not content to saturate one small area with the gospel at the expense of the rest of the world. He had a strategy for reaching the entire Roman Empire. 'But now that there is no more place for me to work in these regions (Jerusalem to Illyricum) and since I have been longing for many years to see you, I plan to do so when I go to Spain' (Romans 15:23–24).

Paul continues to explain his itinerary in this chapter. In his mind he visualized every major city he would stop at on his way to Rome. He longed to eventually win the people of this influential capital city to Christ (just as I long to see London and all of Britain hear the voice of God). But beyond Rome, Paul ultimately wanted to reach the entire known world with the Gospel of Jesus Christ.

Like Paul, our vision as Christians should be 'to win as many people as possible to Jesus Christ throughout the world.' That is part of my team's statement of vision and reason for existence. Paul didn't apologize for actively and aggressively evangelizing the masses from city to city in any way possible, and neither should we.

Evangelism is not an option in the Christian life. Paul admitted: 'Yet when I preach the Gospel, I cannot boast, for I am compelled to preach. Woe to me if I do not preach the Gospel!' (1 Corinthians 9:16). Whether by preaching or praying, travelling around the globe or speaking to those next door, we all should have a part in winning the world to Jesus Christ.

STEP 46

The Fires of Revival

The Apostle Paul's desire to win the world to Jesus Christ always challenges me. Despite the stonings, beatings and other hardships he endured, he sought to fan the fires of revival still brighter.

Paul used strategic thinking to carry out his ministry. His missionary journeys were carefully planned to saturate major cities and provinces with the Gospel of Jesus Christ. He never considered it carnal or beneath his dignity to make such plans.

Even though Paul had a definite strategy to win his generation to Christ, he wasn't bound to it. He remained sensitive to the Spirit's leading. You remember how the Spirit compelled him to go to Macedonia, for instance, even though he had other plans (Acts 16).

This is an exciting concept to me. On the one hand, God intends for us to use logical, strategic planning in fulfilling the Great Commission. But on the other hand, if we are sensitive to the promptings of the Spirit, God can redirect our plans when necessary. One doesn't cancel out the need for the other.

Like Paul, we need to think strategically if the whole world is to hear the voice of God. I believe the nation that could perhaps best fan such a movement of God worldwide would be Britain itself. But first her people need to once again hear and believe God's voice themselves.

After studying the lives of Paul and other great evangelists in church history, I am convinced that God is using evangelistic missions or campaigns to touch millions of lives and bring multiplied thousands into the kingdom of

God. I am equally convinced that God uses other methods as well.

That one form of evangelism is in God's eyes superior to another is a serious theological flaw being heralded by some twentieth century critics. Paul said, 'I have become all things to all men so that by all possible means I might save some' (1 Corinthians 9:22). Witnessing to a friend is no better or worse than preaching to a multitude. God does the work, no matter what method we use. It is through the power of the Holy Spirit and by God's grace that people are saved.

The Scriptures repeatedly testify that God moves both individuals and multitudes of individuals—often after the church experiences a fresh touch of the hand of God. We praise God for what he is doing here in Britain through Christians like you and me who are working together to proclaim the good news of Jesus Christ.

I sincerely believe that God has not abandoned Britain. Yes, I am well aware that the last great movement of God in this land occurred in 1904–5. And yes, I know that it was limited to southern Wales for the most part. But why do we always have to read about revivals of the past? Why can't we *live* revival in our own flesh and blood?

As Evan Roberts—the 'Silent Evangelist' of the Great Welsh Revival—reminded each audience to whom he spoke, God will only pour out the fires of revival on Britain when four things happen:

1. public confession of Jesus Christ as Saviour
2. confession of every known sin
3. the forsaking of every doubtful activity
4. prompt, complete obedience to the Spirit.

If these four things take place in lives throughout this land, the fires of revival could spread into the other Commonwealth nations and indeed into the whole world. What must it take before the revival starts—with you?

STEP 47

Dream Great Dreams

When I was about 17 years old and beginning to take the word of God seriously, one verse really bothered me. I just couldn't believe it meant what it said. I checked other translations to see if I could find a better rendering. But the verse says essentially the same thing in each version.

Jesus Christ declared in that verse, 'I tell you the truth, anyone who has faith in me will do what I have been doing' (John 14:12)

That is a fantastic, almost incredible promise, but there it is. It came from the lips of the Lord Jesus and has been proven many times. Have you proved it true in your own life?

As a teenager growing up in Argentina, I can remember how frustrated I felt about evangelizing the unsaved. 'There are millions of people in this country alone,' I thought. 'Then there's the entire continent. Then the whole world. Yet, here we sit, Sunday after Sunday, the same people doing the same thing. We have to reach out.'

So, several of us began to pray together. 'Lord, get us out of here. Do something. Use us.' Slowly, in my heart and in the hearts of the others, a vision began to grow. A vision of reaching millions of people.

Some of my dreams were so wild I didn't tell anyone except my mother about them, and I didn't even tell her all of them. She encouraged us, saying, 'Come on. You don't need a special message from the Lord. He gave the order centuries ago to preach the good news to everyone.

So go. Don't keep waiting for more instructions.'

So we began to evangelize slowly, in a small way. Now I am constantly amazed how the Lord has fulfilled so many of our great dreams in only twenty years. 'Praise the Lord,' we say. 'It actually happened.'

While Christ was here among us, he deliberately limited himself to three years of ministry in Palestine—to a small area for a short time—before dying and rising from the dead to save us.

Today Christ is calling you to dream great dreams because anyone who believes in him can do the great works he did. How is that possible? The key to this promise is two-fold.

First, because Christ was going to the Father, he would send the Holy Spirit to dwell in us. Now that the Spirit dwells in us as believers, Christ does his works *through us!*

Second, Christ adds a condition to his promise. 'Anyone who has *faith in me* shall do what I have been doing.' The Lord challenges us to have faith—not necessarily to have more faith, but faith in him. It is an on-going faith. The Williams translation puts it this way:

> He who continues to believe in me will also do the works that I do.

Have you stopped seeing great things happen in your life? Perhaps you have stopped believing that God can work in a mighty way even in our generation.

What limits the work of God here on earth? Is God somehow incapable of reviving the churches in Britain? Of turning the hearts of multiplied thousands to himself? Of causing the fires of revival to spread throughout this country and beyond? Of course not!

God has chosen to limit his works, however, to those things we trust him to do through us.

STEP 48

Plan Great Plans

We meet bored people all the time—even bored Christians. They may seem busy, but their days are filled with life's routine, ordinary chores.

As new Christians, we are thrilled by the promises of God. We get excited about answers to prayer. The biographies and books of great men and women of God challenge us to act on our faith.

But as time goes by, sometimes we become hard and cynical. We lose the joy of the Christian life and become bored. We hear of something wonderful that God is doing and say, 'Oh,' as if it is nothing!

The Lord Jesus Christ challenges us to abandon our complacency when he says: 'I tell you the truth, anyone who has faith in me will do what I have been doing. He will do even greater things than these, because I am going to the Father' (John 14:12).

The Lord doesn't intend us to sit idly and simply dream of what could happen for his glory. He wants us to plan great plans so that those dreams will come true!

Someone has well said, 'We believe the Lord can do anything, but we expect him to do nothing.' Often, several years after a person commits his life to Christ he doubts God instead of continuing to trust him for bigger things. He makes no plans for the future bigger than himself.

In order for God to use us again, we need to confess this unbelief and say, 'Lord Jesus, renew my vision of your power. Renew my confidence in your abilities. Renew my trust in your resources.' Then dream and plan again.

William Carey encountered boredom and doubt when he proposed sending missionaries from Britain to evangelize the rest of the world. Older Christians told him to give up his preposterous ideas. But in explaining his dreams and plans Carey wrote: 'Expect great things from God, attempt great things for God.' That statement became the creed of the modern missionary movement as men and women followed Carey's example and went to the ends of the earth with the saving message of Christ's gospel.

God burdened my own heart to win as many people as possible to Jesus Christ—first in my own city, then in my country, then in all of Latin America. Now, by God's grace, we are seeking to let the whole world hear the voice of God.

With that dream, our Team plans to reach the masses using large evangelistic campaigns in various cities. And by God's grace, we are seeing some of our dreams coming true!

What about you? Are you expecting great things from God? Or are you sitting around? If it's true that the Lord Jesus Christ wants the gospel preached world-wide, then we can't remain passive.

Dream a little. Envision the three thousand million people who have never heard the Gospel in this generation. How could God use you to share Christ at work, at school, in your neighbourhood—and beyond? Make specific plans of action. Attempt great things for God today!

STEP 49

Pray Great Prayers

I have a wealthy friend in Latin America who loves the Lord and loves television evangelism. Many times he's told me, 'Luis, any time you have an evangelistic campaign, I'll pay for one night of television. If I can, I'll pay for two or three nights.'

It's nice to have a friend like that! He's a marvellous person. But to be frank with you, I have the hardest time calling him. He's even told me to reverse the charges. Every once in a while he calls me. 'Hey, don't you have any campaigns going? You haven't called me. Don't you need any money?'

Well, of course we have campaigns going and of course we need money to broadcast the gospel. But for some reason I'm very hesitant to call him.

We're like that with the Lord. He doesn't simply challenge us to dream great dreams and plan great plans. He adds: 'And I will do whatever you ask in my name, so that the Son may bring glory to the Father. You may ask me for anything in my name, and I will do it' (John 14:13–14).

What an incredible promise! God wants us to ask him for anything. Yet we hum and haw and beat around the bush. 'Ask me,' the Lord says. 'What are you waiting for?'

When my youngest son was only six, like all six-year-olds, he had a million requests. He asked me for some of the strangest things. Yet, I loved to have him come and ask me. Some of his requests were too much, of course, but I didn't mind. Generally, if I could afford what he wanted, I gave it to him. He's my son.

Our heavenly Father also wants us to come to him with our requests. He delights to give good gifts to those who ask him (Matthew 7:11).

Notice again what the Lord stresses in John 14:13 'Ask in my name, so that the Son may bring glory to the Father.' He challenges us to draw on his infinite resources by asking him in his name for anything that would glorify God. Isn't this our ultimate goal in life?

'I will do whatever you ask...' I have claimed that promise many times during my life. One of my first requests was for a coin so I could get a bus ride to work in Argentina. God didn't miraculously drop the coin out of heaven, but he did supply a ride to work in an unusual way.

God has continued to answer many prayers—prayers for big decisions, desperate needs, safety, personnel, wisdom. Answers to these prayers, whether big or small, have caused my faith to grow and grow.

'Prayer is not conquering God's reluctance, but taking hold upon God's willingness,' as Phillips Brooks said. God already knows our dreams and plans. He doesn't say, 'Sell me, convince me!' He merely says, 'Ask.'

STEP 50

Obey Great Commands

The sign on the stage proclaimed, 'The Motionless Man: Make Him Laugh. Win $100.' The temptation was irresistible. For three hours boys and girls, men and women performed every antic and told every joke they could dream up. But Bill Fuqua, the Motionless Man, stood perfectly serene and still.

Fuqua, current Guinness Book of World Records champion at doing nothing, appears so motionless during his routines at shopping malls, fairgrounds and amusement parks that he's sometimes mistaken for a mannequin.

He discovered his unique talent at the age of 14 while standing motionless in front of a Christmas tree as a joke. A woman touched him and exclaimed, 'Oh, I thought it was a real person.'

Doing nothing is really impossible—even for the Motionless Man. Fuqua attributes his feigned paralysis to hyper-elastic skin, an extremely low pulse rate and intense concentration. He may not laugh at your jokes, but he readily admits he still has to breathe and blink—occasionally.

The Motionless Man reminds me of some Christians who sit still or stand around when they should be acting, speaking, moving. Do people question whether or not you're a real Christian? How can we follow Christ and remain passive at the same time?

The first step in the Christian life is confessing 'Jesus is Lord' (Romans 10:9). As we mature, we understand more fully who Jesus really is—the King of kings and Lord of lords (1 Timothy 6:15). We discover that the day is coming when every tongue shall confess that Jesus Christ is Lord (Philippians 2:11). We realize that God the Father has given him supremacy over all creation (Colossians 1:18).

Every subsequent step in the Christian life involves obeying Jesus as Lord. The apostle John tells us, 'We know that we have come to know him if we obey his commands' (1 John 2:3). To the degree that we know and believe that Jesus is Lord, to that degree we obey him. The Bible calls this 'the fear of the Lord'.

The fear of the Lord implies a deep reverence and awe of God—and a corresponding response of obedience. 'Blessed is the man who fears the Lord, who finds great delight in his commands' (Psalm 112:1).

The Lord Jesus calls us not only to dream great dreams, plan great plans and pray great prayers, but to obey his great commands. 'If you love me, you will obey what I command' (John 14:15). The Lord's commands are always great. He never gives little, puny suggestions.

Listen to his last words before his ascension: 'All authority in heaven and on earth has been given to me.' He is Lord of lords.

> Therefore go and make disciples of all nations, baptising them in the name of the Father and of the Son and of the Holy Spirit, and teaching them to obey everything I have commanded you. And surely I will be with you always, to the very end of the age' (Matthew 28:18–20).

As Lord, he has given us a great commission.

The Lord has not called us to sit around motionless. He's called us to action! Let's move ahead and enjoy the excitement of obeying him and watching people come into his kingdom.

STEP 51

The Unfinished Task

Imagine what would happen if every man, woman and child in Britain heard the Gospel of Jesus Christ clearly proclaimed and committed their lives to him this year.

Why, every newspaper around the world would take notice! Every radio station would report, 'The greatest revival of all time.' Every television news broadcast would discuss the dramatic reformation taking place here.

But our work would *not* be finished. What about the new children? What about the future immigrants? And what about the more than three thousand million people who have never heard a clear presentation of the Gospel?

Statistics overwhelm us. So let's think about the specific individuals we have met who have never committed their lives to Christ. Who comes to mind? Then think about the crowds you see in the cities—at the train stations, in the streets, everywhere. How do you feel when you think about them?

Scripture tells us that when Jesus saw the crowds, 'He had compassion on them, because they were harassed and helpless, like sheep without a shepherd' (Matthew 9:36).

The greatest dangers we face as Christians are cynicism and a cool detachment. 'Oh, yes, so more than three thousand million people don't know Christ. That's too bad.' We must not forget the actual people—including those we know and love—behind that number who live 'without hope and without God in the world' (Ephesians 2:12).

The Lord pointed out the urgency of our task by reminding his disciples, 'The harvest is plentiful, but the workers are few' (Matthew 9:37). We must sense the urgency of our time. How long must people wait before they hear the Gospel? How many more generations must pass before some parts of the world hear the message of Christ for the first time?

It's exciting to see that in most of the so-called Third World today there is a tremendous harvest. Several nations in Latin America and Africa could become 51 per cent Christian within 15 years. And God is at work in Asia as well. Right now the doors are open as perhaps never before in history. Mass communication has made it possible to reach even 'closed' nations with the message of life. All of this is before us now, but it could pass in such a short time.

Our task is urgent. That's why Christ commanded his disciples, 'Ask the Lord of the harvest, therefore, to send out workers into his harvest field' (Matthew 9:38). Our Bibles end the chapter right there, but don't stop reading! In the next five verses the Lord gave his disciples authority and sent them out into the harvest. The twelve became an answer to their own prayer!

In order to finish the task we must have the authority of God that comes from a holy life. Paul told Timothy, 'God did not give us a spirit of timidity, but a spirit of power, of love and of self-discipline' (2 Timothy 1:7). I like to think of this as holy boldness.

The unfinished task of winning the world to Christ is enormous. Are you willing to gain compassion for the unsaved and a sense of urgency in reaching them for Christ? Are you available to God to serve with holy boldness as a worker in his harvest? Let's press on to finish the task set before us.

STEP 52

The Most Important Decision

As Christians, we all can look back to the time in our lives when we made a commitment to Christ. I made that crucial decision while attending a two-week summer camp in the mountains of Argentina.

Charles Cohen, one of my teachers at the British boarding school I attended as a boy, organized the camp each summer. My tent counsellor's name was Frank Chandler.

Every night of the week during summer camp, Mr Chandler would wake up one boy, get him out of bed, and—with a Bible in one hand and a torch in the other—take the boy outside. There, under the stars, he would sit down with the boy and lead him to faith in Christ.

Even though I felt guilty for my sins, and knew I needed to make a Christian commitment, I didn't want to face up to the issue with anyone. But eventually every other boy had talked to Mr Chandler. When he came into the tent that last night of camp, I knew why!

I pretended I was asleep, thinking he would go away. It didn't work. 'Come on, Palau,' he said, 'get up.' I didn't know it, but this was going to be the best night of camp.

We went outside and sat down on a fallen tree. 'Luis,' Mr Chandler asked, 'are you a Christian or not?'

I said, 'I don't think so.'

'Well, it's not a matter of whether you think so or not. Are you or aren't you?'

'No, I'm not.'

'If you died tonight, would you go to heaven or hell?'

I sat quiet for a moment, a bit taken aback, and then said, 'I'm going to hell.'

'Is that where you want to go?'

'No,' I replied.

'Then why are you going there?'

I shrugged my shoulders. 'I don't know.'

Mr Chandler then turned in his Bible to Romans and read: 'If you confess with your lips, Luis, that Jesus is Lord and believe in your heart, Luis, that God raised him from the dead, you, Luis, will be saved. For man believes with his heart and so is justified, and he confesses with his lips and so is saved' (Romans 10:9–10 RSV).

He looked back at me. 'Luis, do you believe in your heart that God raised Jesus from the dead?'

'Yes, I do,' I replied.

'Then what do you have to do next to be saved?'

I hesitated so Mr Chandler had me read Romans 10:9 once more—'If you confess with your mouth "Jesus is Lord"...you will be saved.'

Mr Chandler put his arm around me and led me in prayer. I opened my heart to Christ right there, out in the rain, sitting on a log, in a hurry, but I made my decision. I was only twelve years old at the time, but I knew I was saved. I had eternal life because Christ said, 'I give them eternal life, and they shall never perish; no-one can snatch them out of my hand' (John 10:28).

I could hardly sleep, I was so excited about committing my life to Christ. After all, it is the most important decision anyone can ever make. Compared to eternal life, all other decisions aren't that important when you think about it.

C. S. Lewis, the famous author and teacher, said it well: 'No man is ready to live life on earth until he is ready for life in heaven.' Together let's proclaim the Gospel wherever the Lord leads us so that as many people as possible can be ready.

Fit for a King

by Sue Barnett

In the physical world, there are ways of promoting life and health, and sadly there are ways of stunting growth and restricting sound development.

With refreshing and practical wisdom Sue Barnett explores the parallel between our bodily life and our spiritual wellbeing. All who read the principles and insights shared here, and apply them to their own lives, will be better equipped to serve the King of kings in their daily lives.

Sue Barnett is a trained PE Teacher. Her Life and Growth seminars are appreciated by women nationwide.

k
Kingsway Publications

The Father Heart of God

by Floyd McClung

What is God like?

Has he got time for twentieth-century men and women?

Does he really care?

In his work with *Youth with a Mission*, Floyd McClung has met many who suffer from deep emotional hurts and fears.

Time and again it has been the discovery of God as Father—perfect and reliable, unlike any human parent—that has brought healing and liberty.

This book is for you...

...if you find it hard to accept God as a loving father, or
...if you know God's love but would like to share his blessing with others more effectively.

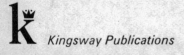

Kingsway Publications

A New Heart
The promise of God to those who believe

by Selwyn Hughes

Is a victorious Christian life possible? Can we know power and purity in our lives, and real faith?

Selwyn Hughes shows how God desires to win our hearts and so enable us to turn his promises into reality.

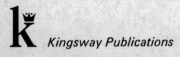

Kingsway Publications

'I want you to get up out of your seat' BILLY GRAHAM

The stories of some who did

As told to Thelma Sangster

With these words Dr Billy Graham has invited people all over the world to come to the front of the crowd in response to his gospel message.

But what happens after they have responded? Do they continue in their faith?

This book traces up to the present day the lives of a handful of people representing the thousands who became Christians as a result of Billy Graham's Crusades in Britain in the fifties and sixties.

As we follow each human drama, we gain a unique insight into how the gospel of Jesus Christ takes hold of lives and changes them. Above all we see proof of God's power at work in people's lives, keeping men and women growing in their faith and triumphant over adversity.

This book is—
— a challenge to Christians to win others and encourage new believers
— an invitation to those who have never considered the tremendous benefits of knowing Jesus to likewise 'get up out of their seats'.

Including an assessment of mass evangelism by ERIC DELVE

Kingsway Publications

How can we believe?

by Robert Dean

How can we believe? Christians and non-Christians face problems raised by the traditional beliefs of Christianity. They cannot be evaded. Robert Dean faces up to the problems with intellectual honesty. His aim is to clear the ground of rational thought to prepare the way for personal commitment. It needs faith to make that commitment, but this book shows that we can have faith without throwing reason out of the window.

The six topics discussed are: Christian faith and science, a loving God and suffering, the reliability of the New Testament, the relevance of Jesus today, answers to prayer and life after death.

k
Kingsway Publications

More than a carpenter

by Josh McDowell

What makes Jesus so different?

He may have been a good man, even a great teacher—but what has he got to do with our lives today?

Josh McDowell thought Christians must be out of their minds. He put them down. He argued against their faith. But then he discovered for himself the truth about Jesus, and experienced his life-changing power.

Here he brings answers for those who are as sceptical as he was—answers for those who have doubts about Jesus, his deity, his resurrection and his claim on their lives.

Over 900,000 copies now in print.

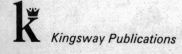

Kingsway Publications

I Believe

by Colin Day

What do Christians believe?

This book is a guide to the basic beliefs of the Christian faith as expressed in the Apostles' Creed.

Far more than a simple list of doctrines, it explores the practical implications of our beliefs, challenging us to a greater depth of Christian commitment in our day-to-day living.

A Falcon Book
Kingsway Publications